GOOD FOOD FOR KIDS

)3

Beyond the jam sandwich

Healthy food ideas for children aged 5 – 12 years

Anne Hillis & Penelope Stone

This book is dedicated to Elizabeth and Felicity who are at the 'jam sandwich' stage, and to Rachel, Rowena and Sarah who have proved beyond doubt that it is possible to 'grow out of' jam sandwiches!

Angus & Robertson
An imprint of HarperCollins*Publishers*, Australia

First published in Australia in 1995

Text Copyright © Anne Hillis and Penelope Stone, 1995

HarperCollins*Publishers*
25 Ryde Road, Pymble, Sydney NSW 2073, Australia
31 View Road, Auckland 10, New Zealand
77–85 Fulham Palace Road, London W6 8JB, United Kingdom
Hazelton Lanes, 55 Avenue Road, Suite 2900, Toronto, Ontario M5R 3L2
and 1995 Markham Road, Scarborough, Ontario M1B 5M8, Canada
10 East 53rd Street, New York NY 10032, USA

National Library of Australia Cataloguing-in-Publication data:

Hillis, Anne.
  Good food for kids: healthy food ideas for children aged 5 to 12 years.

  Includes index.
  ISBN 0207 187916

  1. Cookery. 2. Schoolchildren – Food. 3. Schoolchildren – Health and hygiene. I. Stone, Penelope.
  II. Title. (Series: Parenting series (Pymble, NSW)).
641.5622

Cover illustration by Paul Stanish
Internal illustrations by Paul Stanish

Printed in Hong Kong

9 8 7 6 5 4 3 2 1
95 96 97 98 99

FOREWORD

Feeding children these days is not an easy task, especially if both parents work, and the competition from heavily advertised 'instant' food is ever-increasing. To do the job successfully, the average parent needs the expert knowledge of a dietitian, the culinary talent of a short-order cook, the creative flair of an advertising agency, all coupled with a masterful skill in psychology! Having a strong belief in the value of healthy eating for both you and your children is also important. There is no better way of teaching your children about nutrition than by setting a good example yourself.

The ages of 5 through to 12 are wonderful ones, when life-long learning about food and its effect on health can occur naturally and effortlessly. It is a period when the physically demanding chores of rearing babies and toddlers are over, yet your children have not yet reached the 'drive-parents-mad' rebellious stage of the teenage. Make the most of this time!

Food-related health problems, however, do occur and need to be addressed, especially when there is a family history of any particular illness. The most common ones are:

• Eating too much food for the amount of physical activity done.
• Being underweight (for a small but worrying group of children).
• Eating the wrong sorts of foods every day (excess saturated fats, excess salt, excess sugar).
• Not eating enough of the right foods like vegetables (universally disliked!), lean meat, fish or milk.
• A lack of fibre, which is linked to constipation in children.

Good Food for Kids covers all the key issues relating to feeding your children, including the ones all of us find hard to cope with, such as fussy eaters, overweight children, snacking, food allergies, stemming the demand for fast foods, and foods to nourish children when they are sick. It also takes away the big headache for many parents — how to get your kids to eat good healthy food.

Like its predecessor, *Breast, Bottle, Bowl*, this book is above all a practical guide for busy parents. With its user-friendly style and helpful tips and boxes, *Good Food for Kids* will give you heaps of ideas for easy meals and snacks, show you how to make food and cooking fun, plus answer your queries with its handy reference section on nutrition terms and problems.

The authors, being both parents and caring professionals, write clearly without an overload of technical talk. Their knowledge and understanding of the pitfalls of this age shines out.

Congratulations to Anne Hillis and Penelope Stone on a second excellent work, and I wish this book every success.

Catherine Saxelby
B.Sc., Grad. Dip. Nutrition & Dietitian (Sydney), MDAA
Nutritionist and Accredited Practising Dietitian

CONTENTS

INTRODUCTION

Recently we met a mother who mentioned that her university student son proudly announced that he was 'into' healthy food! Son, mother explained, had for the past 12 years, eaten jam sandwiches for lunch — every day! If mum packed anything else it was not eaten. The change in heart came about because it is not considered trendy to take jam sandwiches for lunch to university!

Despite your good intentions during a child's babyhood, there comes a time when the child will decide what he will and won't eat. Sometimes it may be far from the ideal food, other times there may be some morsel of healthiness! Jam sandwiches may not be nutritionally perfect on one hand but on the other hand, sandwiches are made from bread — an excellent food. Lunch is also important so if the alternative to eating jam sandwiches for lunch means no lunch at all, then jam sandwiches are perfectly acceptable. After all, jam sandwiches are only part of one meal or snack over the whole day.

Children in the ages 5–12 years encounter many influences and influencers which have a great impact on their future as adults. Poor eating during the primary school years may cause heart disease, high blood pressure and high cholesterol problems later in life. It is difficult for a 6 year old child to imagine being old, so nutrition information needs to be relevant to what is happening *now*!

Kids hate feeling sick and enjoy playing with friends and having fun. Tummy aches and toothaches are not very pleasant and can mostly be prevented.

This book is for parents and their children to learn about healthy eating together. The meals in the easy recipe section remove the boredom of 'What can I eat?' and are quicker to prepare than driving down to the takeaway shop — as well as saving you money! Older primary school children will enjoy preparing some of the simple recipes.

As working mothers, we have been through the trials and tribulations of feeding kids in the 5–12 year age group — in fact one of us is still going through it and will continue to do so for quite some time to come. As parents it is our responsibility to teach our children how to eat healthily so as to achieve at school, work and play.

Exercise is the other half of the health equation for children. Do things together as a family — you only have your children for a very short time, so make the very most of it. Our exercise ideas in Chapter One are fun, don't cost anything and will keep parents fit too. We hope that you enjoy this book as well as finding it easy to use. Keep the book handy on the kitchen shelf so that when you run out of ideas, help is at hand. Remember, healthy children grow up to be healthy adults!

Note: We have used 'he' and 'him' in reference to your child and 'she' and 'her' when referring to mother. This makes the book less cumbersome to read. As we only have daughters you can see that we are unbiased in doing this!

CHAPTER ONE

HEALTHY FOOD, HEALTHY KIDS, HEALTHY ADULTS

Getting off to a good start!

You have survived the baby and toddler stages and your child is now going to school. It is to be hoped that any fussy eating has also gone but there will be times when children will be tired, irritable and not necessarily in the mood to eat the food you have prepared. The best teacher of healthy eating is *you*. There has been quite a bit of research to show that children are most influenced by their parents and their eating habits are well-established by the time they are going to school.

Why is healthy food so important?

- It's important to 'get it right the first time'. By teaching your children to eat properly you can avoid them having to 'unlearn' bad habits later in life.
- There is alarming evidence that many children are overweight, are anaemic, suffer from constipation and have high cholesterol problems. All these can be treated and prevented by eating healthily.

- A healthy diet is much cheaper — compare the cost of fruits and vegetables (fresh, canned or frozen) with the cost of packaged crisps, chocolate bars, muesli bars, and other packaged snack foods — you will be surprised at how much money you can save by eating good food. Another cost saving is in medical bills and, if you are a working parent, time lost from work to stay home to look after sick children. Healthy eating promotes good health and reduces the incidence of being sick.
- Your children will be energetic, happy and feel great. A joy to live with (mostly!).
- Your children will cope with the demands of school — their concentration in the classroom will be better and they will have more energy to cope with a busy day.

Benefits of starchy foods

Throw away your old attitudes about starchy foods such as bread, breakfast cereals, pasta, rice and potatoes as being stodgy and fattening. Latest research shows that starchy foods have many positive benefits, including protection against cancer.

Children who cut back on fat often do not replace it with the low-fat starchy foods necessary to meet their daily kilojoule needs for growth. Fruit and vegetables do not supply the daily amount of starch the body needs, so encourage your child to snack and dine on starchy foods.

Healthy parents are important too

The table below, 'What and how much should you eat each day?', is a guide to help parents eat healthy food. Remember that you are your child's best teacher. You may need to adjust the food quantities to suit your energy needs. If you are a very active adult then eat more bread, cereals, fruit and vegetables.

WHAT AND HOW MUCH SHOULD YOU EAT EACH DAY?		
FOOD GROUP	**SIZE OF SERVE**	**NUMBER OF SERVES**
Bread and cereals Provide dietary fibre, carbohydrates, protein, vitamins, minerals and kilojoules.	1 slice bread ½ roll or muffin (include wholegrain/wholemeal varieties for dietary fibre) 2 cracker biscuits ½ cup (90 g/3 oz) cooked rice or pasta 1 bowl breakfast cereal (wholegrain and porridge are best)	4
Fruit	1 piece fruit ½ cup (125 ml/4 fl oz) fruit juice	2
Vegetables Provide dietary fibre, carbohydrates, vitamins (particularly vitamin C), minerals and kilojoules.	½ cup (100 g/3½ oz) starchy vegetables (e.g. potatoes, peas, pumpkin, carrot, parsnip, sweet corn) 1 cup (120 g/4 oz) all other vegetables	5
Dairy foods Provide calcium, protein, vitamins, minerals and kilojoules. Choose reduced-fat varieties.	1 cup (250 ml/8 fl oz) milk 1 slice (30 g/1 oz)cheese 1 tub (200 g/6 ½ oz) yoghurt	4
Meat and meat alternatives Include nuts, beans and eggs. Provide iron, protein, vitamins, minerals and kilojoules.	1 small slice lean meat (veal, pork, beef, lamb, chicken, turkey) 1 medium fillet fish, grilled or steamed 1 small can (100 g/3½ oz) salmon or tuna 1 egg 1–2 tablespoons peanut butter ¼ cup (40 g/1½ oz) nuts ½ cup (100 g/3½ oz) beans, lentils	2
Fats and oils Provide fatty acids, vitamins and kilojoules.	1 tablespoon salad or cooking oil, salad dressing, mayonnaise, butter, cream, margarine or sour cream	1

See the tables in Chapter Two 'Ages and Stages' (page 15) and compare the quantities of food that you and your child will need. Because your child is growing you may notice that he will need more food than you!

Nutrients in a nutshell

WHAT ARE THEY AND WHY ARE THEY IMPORTANT?

Energy

Your child will get all his energy or kilojoules from a variety of foods from the food groups. Sometimes he will be extra hungry if he has been playing sport or is going through a growth spurt. At other times he will not be as active or growing as fast so will not need as much food. Let your child eat according to his appetite and energy requirements. The quantities referred to in 'Ages and Stages' (page 15) are approximate amounts of food needed to support your child's energy needs.

Protein

Protein is vital for growing new tissue and bones and increased blood supply. It is not necessary to eat large lumps of meat — milk, cheese, eggs, and nuts are all good protein sources. By including lots of fruit, vegetables and bread to provide energy, protein can be used for growth rather than for energy.

Fat

After the age of 5 years, you can change your child over to reduced-fat dairy foods. Up until this time, fat has been very important for normal growth of younger children and while it is still necessary, less

of it is needed. Foods such as fruits, vegetables, bread and cereals will provide more of your child's energy requirements. Prepare food with very small amounts of added fats and oils and remember that some foods such as some biscuit varieties, chocolate, crisps, even some mueslis are prepared with added fat. Taking care now will prevent a lot of problems later on in life. Think about how hard is it for adults to reduce the fat in their diets. If the habit has not started in childhood it will be much easier to prevent diseases such as heart disease, some cancers and so on.

MINERALS

Minerals are found in food in adequate quantities but three need special mention.

Iron

Iron is essential to prevent anaemia — a condition where there are not enough red blood cells to keep the child healthy. An anaemic child is tired all the time and has difficulty coping with school and life in general. An anaemic child is more prone to infections and generally can be quite ill. Meat, chicken and green vegetables are excellent sources of iron. However, nutrition being the confusing science that it is, not all iron is equally absorbed in the same way from all foods. Popeye and his spinach made us think how strong we would be by eating spinach but to get the same amount of iron from a small steak we would have to eat 7 cups of boiled spinach! (If you hate spinach this is somewhat daunting!) This is because there are other naturally occurring chemicals and nutrients in green vegetables which stop most of the iron being absorbed. These chemicals do not occur in meat so meat and chicken are the best sources of iron in our diets.

Another interesting fact about iron is that when meat is included in a meal with green vegetables the meat helps the absorption of more iron from the vegetables. Vitamin C is also necessary to help the absorption of iron. This is another reason why vegetables and meat should be eaten together as vegetables are a good source of vitamin C. A small serve of meat each day with green vegetables will ensure that your child has adequate amounts of iron.

Calcium

Childhood is a time of rapid growth, especially for the bones. Haven't you noticed that you are always letting down hems or having to replace clothes? Feet seem to grow at an alarming rate until the age of 12 or 13 years. It has been known for a child to grow out of shoes in 6 weeks. There's a lot to be said for children going around with bare feet! The best sources of calcium are dairy foods. Include low-fat varieties of milk, cheese or yoghurt at each meal as a way of ensuring that your child is getting enough. Bone development starts before birth and continues until late teens. While genetics play an important role in the development of osteoporosis, nutrition and exercise during childhood help develop healthy bones. It is known that a good intake of dairy foods during childhood provides strong bones in adulthood. A good calcium intake now may reduce the risk of osteoporosis later in life.

Zinc

Zinc is an essential mineral for normal growth. Fortunately zinc is found in foods which are good sources of iron and calcium.

VITAMINS

Vitamins are divided into two groups called fat soluble and water soluble.

Fat soluble vitamins

Fat soluble vitamins are A, D, E and K and are, as their name suggests, found in foods containing fats. They are also found in other forms.

Vitamin A is important for normal vision and general good health. It is also found in the diet as Beta carotene which is converted into vitamin A in the body. Beta carotene is found in green, red and orange vegetables and fruit.

Vitamin D is important because it helps calcium to be absorbed. There is a substance in our skin which produces Vitamin D when the sun's ultraviolet rays touch the skin. Take care that your child is not out in the hot direct sun causing skin damage, but rather outside playing in early morning or late afternoon in filtered sunlight. Milk and dairy foods are also good sources of vitamin D.

Vitamin E is found in animal foods such as eggs, fish, meat. It is important as it protects our cells from damage. Deficiency of this vitamin is very rare.

Vitamin K is important for normal blood clotting and is produced in the intestine by the action of certain bacteria. The best food sources are green leafy vegetables but it is found in smaller amounts in a variety of foods.

Water soluble vitamins

Water soluble vitamins include the B group of vitamins and vitamin C.

The B group are destroyed by heat or cooking and need to be eaten every day. A healthy diet negates the need for supplements. There are quite a number of vitamins in the B group. The most well-known are thiamine, riboflavin and niacin. A wide variety of foods each day, including fruit and vegetables, bread, cereal, meat and dairy foods, ensures that your child has plenty of the B group vitamins.

Vitamin C is found in many fruits, especially citrus and berry fruits, as well as vegetables including potatoes. A small glass of juice will provide two to three times the daily required amount of vitamin C. Most children in developed countries have more than adequate amounts of vitamin C.

Exercise – the other half of the health equation

It seems that nowadays we have to make a conscious effort to exercise. At one time all kids either had to walk to school or ride a bike. Today no parent feels confident about the safety of our roads and children are driven to school, driven to sporting activities, dancing lessons, the shops, and so on. Daily exercise, as part of daily living, seems to occur a lot less than it did years ago, except perhaps in country areas where children have access to more outdoor activities. You may need to take definite steps to increase your child's activity level, particularly if your child enjoys sedentary activities such as watching TV and reading.

TEN TIPS TO BEING MORE ACTIVE

1. Put on an exercise video and do the exercises together — what a giggle!

2. Go for a long 'nature' walk through the park. Write out a list of things to collect or see, for example ten things starting with F — feather, football, flower, frog.

3. Encourage your child to join an activity club.

4. Have skipping 'competitions'.

5. Join in bike riding weekends.

6. Put on some popular music and dance.

7. Have competitions to clean the house (with prizes of course!).

8. Encourage your child to participate in chores. This helps you as well as providing exercise.

9. Take up swimming lessons as a family.

10. Buy a dog and take it for a walk every day.

WHY IS EXERCISE SO IMPORTANT FOR KIDS?

Kids are meant to be active, but the minute they start school they are expected to sit still! Encourage exercise as a part of normal development.

• Exercise is a good way to relax — it helps children to get rid of the fidgets.

• Regular exercise is necessary for good growth and development.

• Overweight in children is not always due to poor eating but often due to poor exercise.

• Kids with a regular activity feel great and are generally happier.

• Getting into the exercise habit now will mean it continues in adulthood.

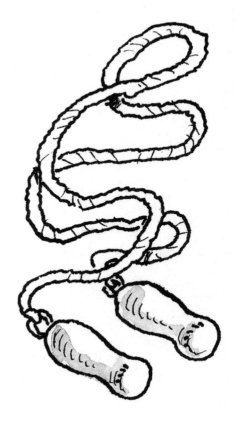

AGES AND STAGES

Your child's development, 5–12 years

Hasn't he grown!

The following tables (pages 16–22) give you an idea of your child's development from age 5 years up to 12 years, the last one to two years of which begins, for most, the exit from childhood as puberty commences.

It's important to remember that these are average guidelines, so do expect some variations. All children are individuals and heredity will largely determine their timetable for development.

The average heights and weights are derived from growth charts used for Australian children. The heights and weights of children are influenced by their parents' height and weight and also by their racial group; for example, children of Asian parents may be smaller than children of European parents. Check with your doctor or dietitian.

Ages and Stages: 5–6 years

AVERAGE WEIGHT

Boys
5 years: 18.5 kg (41 lb)
6 years: 20.5 kg (45 lb)

Girls
5 years: 18 kg (39½ lb)
6 years: 19.5 kg (43 lb)

AVERAGE HEIGHT

Boys
5 years: 110 cm (3 ft 8 in)
6 years: 116 cm (3 ft 11 in)

Girls
5 years: 108.5 cm (3 ft 7 in)
6 years: 115 cm (3 ft 10 in)

DEVELOPMENT

- Most can skip, jump, climb well, run, balance, dance and hop briefly.
- Develops coordination and skills for writing.
- Relatively short legs and large head in proportion to height.
- Becoming leaner.
- Leg length makes them poor at leaping and running fast.
- Knows right from left, ties shoelaces, gives age, knows morning from afternoon.
- Dresses self, throws ball but has difficulty catching it.
- Likes to climb up and down monkey bars or small trees.
- Begins to seek friends outside family; develops social skills. Real playing with friends.
- Shares interests and ideas with family. Practical, inquiring, serious minded.
- Has definite food likes and dislikes. Uses knife and fork well. Good appetite.

DIFFERENCES — BOYS AND GIRLS

Boys
- Slightly taller, less plump, more muscular. More weight from muscle.
- Chunky forearms.
- Right hemisphere of brain more developed, for recognising/remembering patterns such as faces, sounds, and for finding way around. Studies show boys have shorter attention span, less concentration, poorer coordination, and are more likely to be uncooperative, irritable and aggressive, but this is accepted as normal.

Girls
- More body weight from fat.
- Generally both sexes similar build.
- Left hemisphere of brain for language, speech, logic more advanced.

Did you know ... Your child's height depends on the genes he inherits from his parents? Tall parents tend to have tall children, though sometimes not as tall as would be expected; short parents have shorter children, though sometimes taller than expected.

Ages and Stages: 6–7 years

AVERAGE WEIGHT

Boys
6 years: 20.5 kg (45 lb)
7 years: 23 kg (50½ lb)

Girls
6 years: 19.5 kg (43 lb)
7 years: 22 kg (48½ lb)

AVERAGE HEIGHT

Boys
6 years: 116 cm (3 ft 11 in)
7 years: 119.5 cm (4 ft)

Girls
6 years: 115 cm (3 ft 10 in)
7 years: 120.5 cm (4 ft)

DEVELOPMENT

- Excitable, changeable.

- Careless when dressing. Untidy.

- Eats, sleeps well. Competent at meal table. Still has likes and dislikes. Often careless spilling food and restless in chair. Will help set and clear table.

- Loves active play.

- Starts to lose first teeth and get molars.

- Starts to read well. Reads and writes numbers. Adds and subtracts single digit numbers.

- Learns to ride bicycle.

- Knows left hand from right.

DIFFERENCES — BOYS AND GIRLS

Boys
- Heavier than girls.

Girls
- *Slightly* taller at 7.

Ages and Stages: 7–8 years

AVERAGE WEIGHT

Boys
7 years: 23 kg (50½ lb)
8 years: 25 kg (55 lb)

Girls
7 years: 22 kg (48½ lb)
8 years: 25 kg (55 lb)

AVERAGE HEIGHT

Boys
7 years: 119.5 cm (4 ft)
8 years: 127 cm (4 ft 2 in)

Girls
7 years: 120.5 cm (4 ft)
8 years: 126.5 cm (4 ft 2 in)

DEVELOPMENT

- Ties a bow, jumps about a metre. Learns to swim.

- Handles knife and fork well. Will try new foods. Good appetite.

- Leaps ahead in reading and will enjoy books. Writes well. Adds, subtracts.

- Mid growth spurt 7–8. Language more developed.

- Still poor 'staying power' and tends to flit, but is curious.

- Helps with chores, e.g. making beds, washing dishes, housekeeping.

- More play with friends. Keeps secrets for friends and no longer tells all to parents.

- Capable of more complex thinking and problem solving.

- More independent. Able to do more tasks by self. Can be reasoned with. Quiet, thoughtful, polite. Has sense of responsibility.

DIFFERENCES — BOYS AND GIRLS

Boys
- Similarity in height and weight between sexes.

Girls
- Continued increase in percentage weight as body fat.

- Slightly taller at 7 but similar height at 8.

- At this age they are physically stronger than boys.

Riboflavin (vitamin B2) and cow's milk

Your child's daily need for riboflavin or vitamin B2 is easily met by consuming cow's milk:

- Boys and girls aged 5–7 years: about 700 ml (24 fl oz) of milk

- Boys aged 8–11 years: about 700 ml (24 fl oz) of milk

- Girls aged 8–11 years: 800 ml (27 fl oz) of milk

- Boys aged 12 years: 1050 ml (34 fl oz) of milk

- Girls aged 12 years: 950 ml (32 fl oz) of milk

Ages and stages: 8–9 years

AVERAGE WEIGHT

Boys
8 years: 25 kg (55 lb)
9 years: 28 kg (61½ lb)

Girls
8 years: 25 kg (55 lb)
9 years: 28.5 kg (63 lb)

AVERAGE HEIGHT

Boys
8 years: 127 cm (4 ft 2 in)
9 years: 132 cm (4 ft 5 in)

Girls
8 years: 126.5 cm (4 ft 2 in)
9 years: 132 cm (4 ft 5 in)

DEVELOPMENT

- Sociable, outgoing, energetic.
- Good appetite. May still have strong food likes and dislikes. Still has some difficulty cutting meat with a knife.
- Best time to learn musical instrument is 8–11 years.
- Most are well-coordinated physically. Play is lively. Likes team sports.
- Have longer legs and shorter bodies so power to run and leap increases.
- Head size is more in proportion to height.
- Reads well. Adds and subtracts 2 or 3 digit numbers. Multiplies single digit numbers.
- Continuing separation from parents and closeness to peers.
- Questions former view of parent as perfect. Realizes parents are humans with shortcomings. This drives them closer to peers.

DIFFERENCES — BOYS AND GIRLS

Boys
- More percentage weight from muscle than fat. By 9 years 46% of weight is muscle compared to 42% in girls.

Girls
- More percentage weight from fat. At 9 girls have 16% of weight as fat compared to boys' 12%.

- Both sexes about same height and weight.

Did you know ... Two cups (500 ml/16 fl oz) of orange juice (only two 250 ml/8 fl oz Tetrapak containers) is equivalent in energy to eating four oranges? Encourage your child to eat fruit rather than juice. He'll not only get all the nutrients including the fibre which is missing in juice, he'll also be more satisfied and 'feel full'.

Ages and Stages: 9–10 years

AVERAGE WEIGHT

Boys
9 years: 28 kg (61½ lb)
10 years: 31.5 kg (69 lb)

Girls
9 years: 28.5 kg (63 lb)
10 years: 32.5 kg (71½ lb)

AVERAGE HEIGHT

Boys
9 years: 132 cm (4 ft 5 in)
10 years: 137 cm (4 ft 6 in)

Girls
9 years: 132 cm (4 ft 5 in)
10 years: 138 cm (4 ft 7 in)

DEVELOPMENT

• Becoming a 'little adult'. Practical, serious, well-mannered. Socially responsible.

• Has opinions about how he or she is treated, and will express opinions about fairness and justice.

• Continues close relationship with peers. Becoming independent of mum and dad.

• Bodies continue to get longer and more compact.

• Develops physical strength.

• Can throw ball in air and clap hands, then catch ball again.

• Likes to play on own as well as in team sports.

• Good table manners. Shows courtesy.

• Has basic skills of reading, writing and multiplying.

DIFFERENCES — BOYS AND GIRLS

Boys
• Stronger hand grip.

• Arm thrust, strength, pull, agility, and balance similar between sexes.

Girls
• Heavier and taller at age 10 than boys.

Did you know ... At 10 years old, boys and girls are about 4 cm (1½ in) taller and 2 kg (4½ lb) heavier than 10 year old boys and girls in 1970? In fact, children and adults of varying ages are about 9 cm (3½ in) taller today than children and adults in 1911! The most likely explanation for this is better nutrition and fewer infectious diseases.

Ages and Stages: 10–11 years

AVERAGE WEIGHT

Boys
10 years: 31.5 kg (69 lb)
11 years: 35 kg (77 lb)

Girls
10 years: 32.5 kg (71½ lb)
11 years: 37 kg (81½ lb)

AVERAGE HEIGHT

Boys
10 years: 137 cm (4 ft 6 in)
11 years: 143 cm (4 ft 9 in)

Girls
10 years: 138 cm (4 ft 7 in)
11 years: 145 cm (4 ft 10 in)

DEVELOPMENT
- A 'little adult'. Cool, calm and collected!
- Can go alone to camps, shops, catches public transport alone.
- Reads well, writes short stories.
- Likes to earn money by doing odd jobs.
- Accepts defeat in sport etc. more easily than when younger.
- Maths skills more advanced.
- Interested in self and defends self against criticism.
- Interested in social issues and the future.

DIFFERENCES — BOYS AND GIRLS

Boys
- Shorter and lighter than girls.

Girls
- More mature than boys. More interested in their appearance. Different interests to boys. Mix with other girls in groups.
- Growth spurt begins about 10–11, two years earlier than boys. Girls are taller and heavier than boys.

Did you know ... Nutrients at risk for children aged 10–12 years are: iron (for girls 12 years), calcium (for girls 10–12 years), and zinc (for boys 12 years and girls 10–12 years)?

AVERAGE WEIGHT

Boys
11 years: 35 kg (77 lb)
12 years: 40 kg (88 lb)

Girls
11 years: 37 kg (81½ lb)
12 years: 41.5 kg (91 lb)

AVERAGE HEIGHT

Boys
11 years: 143 cm (4 ft 9 in)
12 years: 149 cm (4 ft 11 in)

Girls
11 years: 145 cm (4 ft 10 in)
12 years: 151 cm (5 ft)

DEVELOPMENT

• Leaving childhood and entering puberty and adolescence.

• Timing of puberty varies. Depends on hereditary, nutrition, physical factors. Average age girls 11, range 9–13. Average age boys 12, range 9–14.

• Puberty characterised by large growth spurt, development of sex organs (ovaries/girls; testes prostate gland, seminal vesicles/boys). Secondary sex characteristics such as breasts, pubic hair. Usually takes 2–5 years.

• Continuing independence, physical and mental development. Becoming 'more adult'. Starts to develop own identity.

• Good appetite.

• 'Growing pains' may occur.

DIFFERENCES — BOYS AND GIRLS

Boys
• At 12 testicles enlarge, scrotum darkens.

• Fine straight pubic hair at base of penis.

• Some boys will have slight breast enlargement which will disappear.

• Growth spurt later than girls. Begin to grow quickly at 13.

• Growth in muscle and hence greater physical strength.

Girls
• Growth spurt earlier than boys. Heavier and taller at age 11 and 12 than boys.

• Hands and feet grow at faster rate than rest of body.

• Breast buds begin, fine straight pubic hair, changing to coarse and curly by about 12.

• Growth of vagina and uterus.

• Increase in body fat.

How much food should your child be eating?

Parents often ask us to give them an idea of how much food their child should be eating. They are particularly interested to know whether he is eating too much or too little! We've calculated the following table (page 24) based on daily energy needs, to give you a rough idea of the quantities of food an average healthy child should be eating to meet his nutrient requirements.

Use it as a guide only. Your child's daily food intake will vary from one day to the next, just like an adult's. Some days he'll eat heaps, other days he'll hardly seem to eat anything. The quantities eaten will also vary from one child to the next depending on activity, size, sex and growth. Children usually eat more during a growth spurt and with the onset of puberty. So don't forget to let them eat more if this is the case. However, ensure a balance of foods from all groups is maintained. If your child is eating too much from one food group it is likely to be at the expense of another and vital nutrients may be missed.

The intakes of breads and cereals, fruits and vegetables are likely to vary most.

Calcium: meeting daily requirements

BOYS AND GIRLS AGED 5–7, AND BOYS AGED 8–11

They need 800 mg of calcium a day, which can be met by eating:

- 700 ml (23 fl oz) of milk or calcium-fortified soy beverage, *or*

- 1 cup (250 ml/8 fl oz) of milk or calcium-fortified soy beverage *plus* 1 slice of cheese (30 g/1 oz) *plus* 1 tub (200 g/6½ oz) of yoghurt.

GIRLS AGED 8–11

They need 900 mg of calcium a day, which can be met by eating:

- 800 ml (27 fl oz) of milk or calcium-fortified soy beverage, *or*

- 1 cup (250 ml/8 fl oz) of milk *plus* 1 slice of cheese (30 g/1 oz) *plus* 1 tub (200 g/6½ oz) of yoghurt *plus* 2 scoops of ice-cream.

BOYS AGED 12

They need 1200 mg of calcium a day, which can be met by eating:

- 1050 ml (35 fl oz) of milk or calcium-fortified soy beverage, *or*

- 300 ml (10 fl oz) carton of milk *plus* 1 tub (200 g/6½ oz) of yoghurt *plus* 2 slices of cheese (60 g/2 oz) *plus* 2 scoops of ice-cream.

GIRLS AGED 12

They need 1000 mg of calcium a day, which can be met by eating:

- 950 ml (32 fl oz) of milk or calcium-fortified soy beverage, *or*

- 300 ml (10 fl oz) carton of milk *plus* 1 tub (200 g/6½ oz) of yoghurt *plus* 1 slice of cheese (30 g/1 oz) *plus* 2 scoops of ice-cream.

APPROXIMATE DAILY FOOD INTAKE FOR CHILDREN 5–12 YEARS

FOOD GROUP	SIZE OF SERVE	AGE	NUMBER OF SERVES
Breads and cereals	1 slice bread ½ bread roll 2 plain savoury biscuits ½–1 cup breakfast cereal ½ cup cooked porridge 1 wheat flake biscuit ½ cup cooked pasta, or rice	5–6 years 6–7 years 7–8 years 8–9 years 9–10 years 10–11 years 11–12 years	Boys 6 serves; girls 5 serves Boys 6 serves; girls 5 serves Boys 7 serves; girls 5 serves Boys 7 serves; girls 5 serves Boys 8 serves; girls 6 serves Boys 8 serves; girls 6 serves Boys 8 serves; girls 7 serves
Fruit	1 piece fruit 125 ml (4 fl oz) fruit juice 2 tablespoons sultanas/raisins 4 pieces dried fruit	5–6 years 6–7 years 7–8 years 8–9 years 9–10 years 10–11 years 11–12 years	Boys 3 serves; girls 2 serves Boys 3 serves; girls 2 serves Boys 3 serves; girls 3 serves Boys 3 serves; girls 3 serves Boys 3 serves; girls 3 serves Boys 3 serves; girls 3 serves Boys 3 serves; girls 3 serves
Vegetables	1 cup cooked vegetables 1 med potato (100 g/3 oz) or ½ cup mashed potato (125 g/ 4 oz) ½ cup carrot slices (60 g/ 2 oz)	5–6 years 6–7 years 7–8 years 8–9 years 9–10 years 10–11 years 11–12 years	Boys 3 serves; girls 3 serves Boys 3 serves; girls 3 serves Boys 4 serves; girls 3 serves Boys 4 serves; girls 3 serves Boys 4 serves; girls 3 serves Boys 4 serves; girls 3 serves Boys 4 serves; girls 3 serves
Dairy foods	200 ml (6½ fl oz) milk 200 g (6½ oz) yoghurt 40 g (1½ oz) cheese 200 ml (6½ fl oz) custard	5–6 years 6–7 years 7–8 years 8–9 years 9–10 years 10–11 years 11–12 years	Boys 3½ serves; girls 3½ serves Boys 3½ serves; girls 3½ serves Boys 3½ serves; girls 3½ serves Boys 3½ serves; girls 4 serves Boys 3½ serves; girls 4 serves Boys 3½ serves; girls 4 serves Boys 3½ serves; girls 4 serves
Meat and meat substitutes	Small serve of lean cooked beef, chicken or fish 1 egg 1 tablespoon peanut butter ½ cup (140 g/4½ oz) baked beans 1 fish finger	5–6 years 6–7 years 7–8 years 8–9 years 9–10 years 10–11 years 11–12 years	Boys 2 serves; girls 2 serves Boys 3 serves; girls 3 serves Boys 3 serves; girls 3 serves Boys 4 serves; girls 4 serves Boys 4 serves; girls 4 serves Boys 4 serves; girls 4 serves Boys 4 serves; girls 4 serves
Fats and oils	2 teaspoons butter, poly/monounsaturated margarine or oil	5–6 years 6–7 years 7–8 years 8–9 years 9–10 years 10–11 years 11–12 years	Boys 2 serves; girls 2 serves Boys 2 serves; girls 2 serves Boys 2 serves; girls 2 serves Boys 2 serves; girls 2 serves Boys 2 serves; girls 2 serves Boys 2 serves; girls 2 serves Boys 3 serves; girls 3 serves
Extras	1 small piece of cake or pastry 1 small packet crisps or similar snack 2–3 sweet biscuits 1 tablespoon jam or honey 4 squares chocolate/5 caramels 1 can (375 ml/12 fl oz) soft drink	These 'Extras' are allowed as a 'treat' from time to time for energy and variety, but preferably *not* on a daily basis. They are high in fat and/or sugar and low in nutrients. Limit to 1 serve per day. Other 'extras' can also be chosen from the food groups above.	

CHAPTER THREE

TASTE, APPETITE, GROWTH

If it doesn't taste good, give it a miss!

Why all this fussiness with food?

Most parents at some stage become exasperated with their child's food refusal and fussiness. Their best efforts to provide healthy nutritious foods are often done in vain.

Recent interviews with 622 parents representing 1061 children found that two out of three children under 12 were fussy eaters and three out of four parents felt irritated, guilty or concerned their children were not eating balanced meals. One third of parents always or sometimes made separate meals for their children. The least liked foods were vegetables and the ages 3–9 years were regarded as the most fussy.

So why do children reject foods adults think are 'good for them'? Are children's tastes different to adults'? Why is there

always room for 'junk' food but never enough for healthy food? Have you ever heard of a child rejecting potato crisps or chocolate?

The answers lie in three areas: taste, appetite and growth.

Taste

If it doesn't taste good, give it a miss! What we eat is determined by taste, smell and texture, not nutrition. So if a food tastes 'yucky', even though it's fabulously nutritious, it won't be eaten.

We have four basic tastes — sweet, sour, bitter and salty. Sensitivity to different tastes occurs on the tongue, with its front and tip being sensitive to sweetness, its side to saltiness and its back to sour and bitter tastes. Other areas around the mouth are also sensitive to taste such as the cheeks, but to a lesser extent than the tongue.

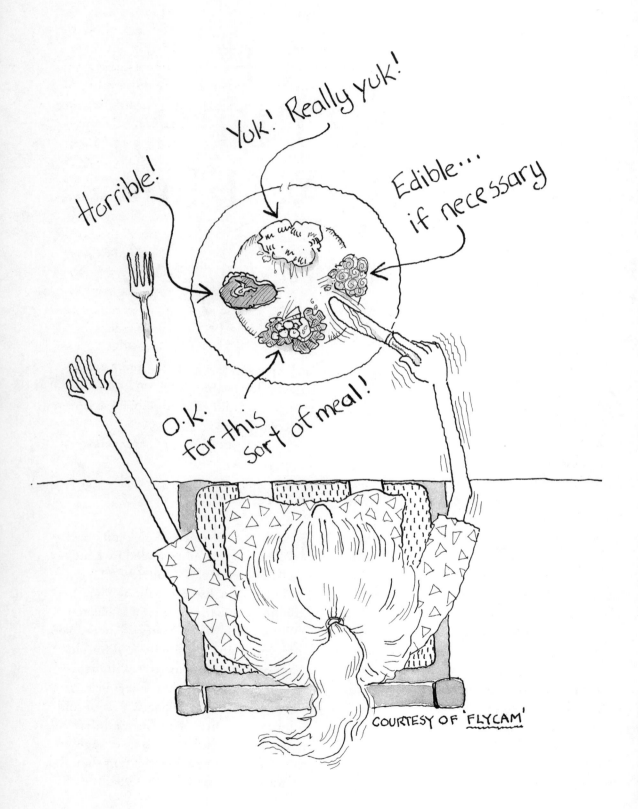

Infants are born with an inherent liking for sweet foods and a dislike for sour or bitter tastes. Breast milk is a sweet milk (much sweeter than cow's milk) and infants readily accept it and other sweet liquids and foods, because the tip of the tongue is most sensitive to sweetness.

Children generally love sweet foods and have a dislike for sour and bitter foods. A liking for sweet foods probably developed during human evolution, and provided a simple way of determining whether foods were safe or unsafe to eat. Sweet foods were generally safe, while bitter foods were an indication that poisons may be present and the food was therefore unsafe.

One of the reasons children probably dislike many vegetables is that they often contain bitter or sour flavours which do not appeal.

Infants and children do taste foods differently from adults because their sense of taste and smell is more highly developed. At birth an infant has about 12,000 taste buds. This number halves by 18 years; by 50 years only about 2000–3000 buds remain. Similarly, our sense of smell declines with age, the number of nerves in the nasal cavity halving by adulthood.

So tastes acceptable to adults will not necessarily be acceptable for children. Most of us remember disliking certain foods as children, and then accepting them as adults (for example olives, anchovies, asparagus, oysters) or loving foods as a child and loathing them as adults (for

example milk chocolate drinks, pre-sweetened breakfast cereals).

We therefore have to be careful not to judge our children's tastes by our own. Watch spices and condiments before you add them to dishes. Encourage your child to help with the meal preparation and to 'taste test' before adding extra flavours.

Many parents worry that feeding children sweet foods will lead to the development of a sweet taste later in life. Parents should relax about the preference for sweet foods as this will decline with age. Severely restricting sweet foods may lead to poor diet and growth. However parents should still be selective as to the sweetened foods they give, ensuring that they contain some nutrients or act as a vehicle for more nutritious foods to be accepted. For example flavoured milk is better than no milk at all; pre-sweetened breakfast cereals served with milk are better than missing breakfast altogether.

But why do our children like takeaways and commercial snack foods but not certain fresh vegetables and fruits?

It all comes back to taste, texture and convenience. Commercial foods and takeaways are popular because they have good flavour, a manageable texture requiring little chewing and they give instant pleasure. As one mother said 'once kids get hooked on pizza everything else is tame'. Advances in food technology have meant that these foods always have a consistent, predictable flavour and texture. Unprocessed foods such as fruits and vegetables are not always consistent in flavour and texture nor always available because Mother Nature cannot make them this way. Apples can vary in flavour and texture with season, and also from one apple to the next.

Children will not eat or be convinced to eat vegetables and fruit simply because 'they are good for you'. They will be eaten only if they have good flavour, texture and give pleasure when eaten.

So what can parents do?

- Choose high quality fresh vegetables and fruits in season. If possible check for flavour and texture before buying. Buy in small quantities at first, then buy more if tasty.
- Take care with cooking (refer to Chapter Nine).
- Try serving vegetables raw or as a salad.
- Try commercial foods. Some children prefer canned, frozen and dried vegetables to the fresh. The nutritional goodness is still there.
- Fresh fruit can be substituted by canned, frozen, or stewed fruit. Snack packs of fruit made with pure fruits are often more acceptable in the lunchbox and easier to eat than fresh.

What about fat?

A preference for fatty foods, unlike sweet foods, does not appear to be innate in children. However children frequently given high-fat foods from an early age soon learn to associate them with a reduction in hunger.

High-fat foods usually contain sugar and salt, flavours liked by young children.

What about salt?

A liking for salty food is not innate but is acquired. Babies happily eat low-salt foods much to the surprise of their parents who find the taste bland and uninteresting. However, as children get older and eat more varied foods they tend to develop a taste for salt. Most snack foods given to children tend to be salty. As too much salt has been associated with high blood pressure and heart disease, and we are eating more than our body needs, foods should be chosen that are low or reduced in salt and the salt shaker removed from the table.

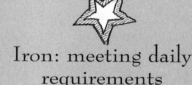

Iron: meeting daily requirements

BOYS AND GIRLS AGED 5–11

They need 6–8 mg of iron a day, which can be met by eating:

- 1 cup of iron-fortified breakfast cereal *plus* 2 lean grilled chops, *or*

  100 g (3 oz) of lean red meat or 2 grilled thick sausages *plus* 3 slices of wholemeal bread.

BOYS AND GIRLS AGED 12

They need 10–13 mg of iron a day, which can be met by eating:

- 1 cup of iron-fortified breakfast cereal, *plus* a small piece of grilled steak (100–150 g/3–4 oz), *plus* 4 slices of wholemeal bread, *plus* ½ cup baked beans.

Appetite and growth

If a healthy child doesn't want to eat, he's simply not hungry. Children's appetites vary and this is very much related to their growth spurts and activity. You'll know when a growth spurt occurs — a child will eat more than you thought and it'll be hard to keep the pantry stocked.

The ages between 5 and 12 years are characterised by a continuing growth in height and weight and most children during these ages have a good appetite. Boys and girls will more than double their weight and increase their height by about 39 cm (15½ in) for boys and 42.5 cm (17 in) for girls.

These are also the playful years when children are full of energy and love physical exercise. Exercise makes for a good appetite.

Children should be encouraged to play and exercise and be discouraged from becoming 'couch potatoes' in front of the TV, which may lead to overweight and lethargy.

Between 5 and 8 years the rate of weight gain is steady at about 2–3 kg (4–6 lb) a year. The most obvious change is in height. Girls 'shoot up' mostly between 6 and 7 years (5.5 cm or 2 in) and boys a year later, between 7 and 8 years (7.5 cm or 3 in). Appetite will increase as the child 'sprouts'.

The most noticeable change in appetite occurs between 9 and 12 years. This is the time when puberty may be beginning or is underway, with gains in height at an average of 6–7 cm (2½–3 in) per year and weight 4–5 kg (9–11 lb) per year. Keep your pantry stocked during this time with healthy snacks (see Chapter Nine) and expect your child to be forever hungry.

CHAPTER FOUR

THE TOOTH FAIRY'S BEEN!

Healthy teeth and gums

From first to permanent teeth

The tooth fairy will be a regular visitor between the years 5 and 12. These are exciting times for children as first (baby) teeth loosen and are gradually replaced with permanent teeth. You'll be surprised to see how children become quite competitive in the 'tooth losing stakes'. To keep up with friends who lose teeth earlier, they often intentionally eat hard foods such as apples to help the wobbly tooth fall out sooner.

Teeth tell a lot about us, particularly our age. Just as you can tell the age of a horse by looking at its teeth, so you can with a child. This is because there are defined ages when tooth development takes place. By 2½ years a child has all his first twenty teeth. Between 3 and 5 years the face grows and the jaw widens to make way for permanent teeth. The growth spurt between 5 and 7 years sees your child lose his baby face.

The first (baby) teeth start to fall out at about age 6. (Remember however, that there are wide individual variations.) When this happens the root of the tooth dissolves until only the crown is left. When it falls away, the crown of the new permanent tooth becomes visible.

There are thirty-two permanent teeth, sixteen in each jaw (as shown in the following diagram, page 32), and each has been developing since birth. The first ones to appear are the four 6 year old molars, two in the upper jaw and two in the lower jaw. Once these molars are in place, the first (baby) teeth will shed in about the same order as they appeared.

By 12½ all permanent teeth will be in place except for the third molars (wisdom teeth) which do not appear for another 5 years or more. Some problems — such as over-crowding, crooked teeth, lower teeth too far forward in relation to upper teeth, second teeth through before first (baby) teeth are lost — may occur as teeth come through. Visit your dentist if you have any concerns.

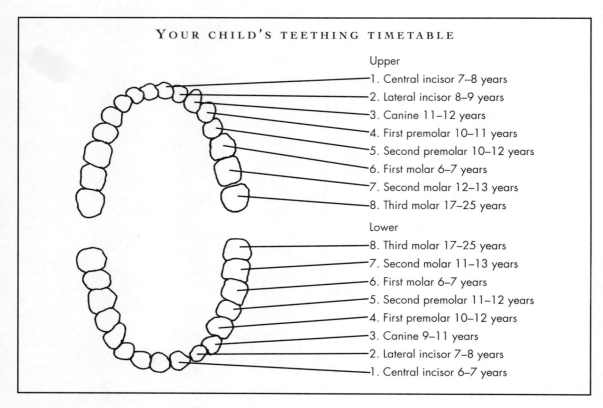

Upper
- 1. Central incisor 7–8 years
- 2. Lateral incisor 8–9 years
- 3. Canine 11–12 years
- 4. First premolar 10–11 years
- 5. Second premolar 10–12 years
- 6. First molar 6–7 years
- 7. Second molar 12–13 years
- 8. Third molar 17–25 years

Lower
- 8. Third molar 17–25 years
- 7. Second molar 11–13 years
- 6. First molar 6–7 years
- 5. Second premolar 11–12 years
- 4. First premolar 10–12 years
- 3. Canine 9–11 years
- 2. Lateral incisor 7–8 years
- 1. Central incisor 6–7 years

Protecting permanent teeth

Teeth not only affect our appearance but help us to speak clearly and chew foods. So it's very important to keep a healthy mouth.

Your child's permanent teeth have to last a lifetime, so it is vital that they are well looked after. Encourage good dental hygiene so that tooth decay and periodontal disease are avoided. Periodontal disease does not involve the teeth, but the gums and the bone supporting the roots of the teeth and results from inadequate cleaning.

Tooth decay occurs when sugars (sucrose, glucose, maltose, lactose, fructose) from foods are converted to acid in the mouth by the natural bacteria present. The acid eats away at the tooth and creates a hole which, when large enough, attacks the root and causes pain. The more frequent the acid attacks the more harm is done.

TIPS FOR KEEPING TEETH AND GUMS HEALTHY

A healthy diet

- Follow the healthy diet guidelines as mentioned in Chapter 2.
- Avoid too many sticky sugary foods such as cakes, biscuits, doughnuts, jam, honey, lollies and chocolates, sweetened breakfast cereals, toasted muesli and health food bars. The more frequent the acid attacks from food the more damage that is done. Avoid between meal snacks of sweet, sticky food.
- Carbonated soft drinks contain a lot of sugar and are very acidic so are harmful to the teeth. Lemon and grapefruit

juices are also very acidic. Consume with meals and drink through a straw, swallowing rapidly to lessen enamel damage.

- Foods protective to the teeth include cheese, milk, yoghurt and peanuts. They increase salivary flow, raise pH so there is less acid to attack teeth, and increase the calcium content of the saliva. Milk proteins and fats also form a protective coating on the surface of the teeth making them less susceptible to acid attack.

- Apples and carrots have a scouring effect that reduces plaque (a film on the teeth in which bacteria convert carbohydrates into acid) formation on biting surfaces. However, apples can still produce acid which causes caries.

- Artificial sweeteners Xylitol, Splenda (sucralose), Nutrasweet (aspartame), and Saccharin do not cause caries.

- Recent research has shown that chewing sugar-free gum for about 20 minutes after a meal or snack can keep teeth and gums healthy. Chewing increases saliva flow which neutralizes the acid from plaque which causes tooth decay. Sugar-free gum may be a protective way to clean teeth after a meal when brushing isn't practical.

Drink fluoridated water

Most water supplies in Australia have added fluoride. Fluoride makes the enamel surface of the tooth stronger so it is resistant to acid attack. It boosts remineralization, and slows or inhibits the production of acids from acid producing bacteria.

Fluoridation of water has led to a dramatic reduction in dental caries in children. Fluoride should be present during the first 14–15 years of life when teeth are forming. If you use a water filter to purify your water, check with the manufacturer that it does not remove fluoride from the water. Carbon filters and ceramic filters do not remove fluoride while ion exchange and reverse acinous filters and distillers do.

If you live in an unfluoridated water area (that is where the natural fluoride content of the water is less than 0.3 mg fluoride per litre) your child will need to take a daily fluoride supplement. For children 3–16 years, 1 mg fluoride per day should be given. Although you can give fluoride directly to your child by tablets or drops, it's just as easy, and definitely more natural, to make up your own fluoridated water for home use. For each litre of water add 1 mg fluoride as tablets or drops (for tropical areas add 1 mg fluoride for each 1.5 litres/48 fl oz of water). Store in the fridge and use throughout the day for drinking, cooking, making drinks etc.

If you do decide to give fluoride daily by drops or tablets, remember that if you forget to give on one day, don't double up on the next. Make sure you keep tablets and drops out of children's reach.

Fluoridated toothpaste is another source of fluoride. Its pleasant taste unfortunately makes some young children regard it as a food. Rather than using a small smear on the brush and spitting it out after use some children use far too much and swallow. Some even eat it as a snack! To avoid your child getting too much fluoride (particularly a child aged 6 years or less), parents should supervise the amount of toothpaste used. Adult fluoride toothpastes can be used by children provided only a thin smear is used and the toothpaste is not swallowed. However, for those children who like to use a lot of toothpaste, swallow it and clean their teeth unsupervised, the use of a low-fluoride or junior toothpaste is suggested up to age 6 years.

Oral hygiene

- Brush teeth regularly after meals and snacks.
- Use a small size toothbrush and a fluoride toothpaste. A low-fluoride toothpaste is recommended up to 6 years if your child tends to ingest toothpaste and brushes unsupervised. While toothpastes today are pleasant tasting, discourage your child from ingesting it. You only need a thin smear on the brush or a dot the size of a pea (see above).
- Supervise brushing. All children need supervision and help with brushing until age 10, as they usually do not have the manual dexterity to do it properly themselves. Ideally, a parent should clean a child's teeth once per day.

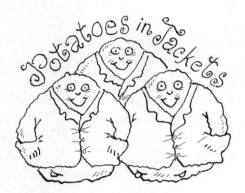

Visit the dentist for regular check ups

Your child should have been seeing a dentist since 2 years of age and so by 5–6 years will be used to going to the dentist. Discuss teeth and mouth care with your dentist.

Did you know ... Not all sweet foods willl cause caries to the same extent? Research shows that the type and form of carbohydrate is important. Soft drinks and chocolate appear not to increase the risk of caries as much as potato crisps, biscuits or sticky lollies. This is because the soft drink and chocolate are easily removed from the mouth whereas the crisps, biscuits and sticky lollies cling to the teeth for a longer time giving bacteria plenty of opportunity to produce acids and thus cavities. Chocolate also contains milk proteins which tend to be protective against fat.

CHAPTER FIVE

DEVELOPING GOOD EATING HABITS

Feel well, eat well

The importance of being a breakfast eater

There is lots of information around on the importance of breakfast — 'But he just won't eat'. We hear this comment often. As parents, and therefore healthy eating educators, we can teach our children to eat breakfast by eating breakfast ourselves.

The non-breakfast eating trend starts in early school days when the child is tired and can't get out of bed. It's quicker and easier often to rush off to school without breakfast. *It is better to be late for school than to miss breakfast!* (Remember that baby with the voracious appetite? He *always* ate breakfast!)

Breakfast is very important and should never be missed. However it doesn't have to be a three-course meal. It can be a nourishing drink. Many people claim that they are not hungry in the morning, but eating breakfast helps you to wake up and this is especially important for a child going to school.

WHY IS BREAKFAST SO IMPORTANT?

- Children who skip breakfast have been found to feel tired and lethargic during the morning and have poor concentration.
- If your child misses breakfast he is missing one-third of his daily nutrients and this can be difficult to catch up.
- Studies have shown that there is an increase in absenteeism from school in children who miss breakfast.

Don't forget that breakfast does not have to be eaten as soon as you get out of bed! Other activities such as dressing, doing morning chores and packing the school bag can be done first. Nor does breakfast have to be traditional breakfast type food. Children enjoy fresh or stewed fruit, custard, yoghurt, leftovers on toast, milk drinks, even good home-made soup as well as the 'usual' breakfast foods such as cereals, toast, eggs, baked beans, milk. See Chapter Nine for some new breakfast ideas.

Snacking

Ideally, children need to snack two to three times a day in order to eat enough food to get sufficient nutrients. However snacking tends to be considered unhealthy by the ill-informed. Why? Because the extra snacks are not included in the day's food intake and are not 'counted'. Snacks do 'count' and are very important sources of nutrients.

Good snack foods are essential for your child's health and wellbeing. Many children are 'grazers' and eat small amounts of food often. This is also a good way to eat provided that the food chosen is healthy.

Suitable snack foods are fruit, cheese, sandwiches, breakfast cereal (many children enjoy a bowl of cereal and milk as a snack after school). For more snack ideas refer to Chapter Nine.

Television advertising

+ magz etc

As parents we must monitor the types of programs our children watch on television and we should also be aware of the types of TV advertising shown during children's popular TV shows. Recent surveys have shown that children can be a strong influence on parents and what they purchase. In some instances this can be OK, but unfortunately many high-fat, high-salt snack foods are advertised during children's peak viewing times.

You should be aware of what your child is watching and take the opportunity to discuss the appropriateness of the food or snack food. Does it fit into the recommended Food Groups? How much does it cost? Of course some advertisements are for healthy foods such as bread, milk and meat, so take the opportunity to discuss healthy food versus unhealthy or junk food advertisements.

The 4 o'clock 'binge'

Most kids are 'starving' when they get home from school so have a range of healthy foods to eat rather than 'empty' foods such as packet crisps and chocolate bars. Your child will indeed be hungry so a mini meal is not out of the question. Nourishing soup, toast, sandwiches, fruit, baked beans on toast, poached eggs, even part of the evening meal can be eaten now. See Chapter Nine for some good ideas on after-school snacks.

Often children are too tired to eat properly at the family meal time but enjoy eating at 4 o'clock. This could be a good time to serve an early dinner followed by some fruit or a small snack at the family meal time. This satisfies the social importance of sitting together at the family meal table, yet provides a substantial meal when your child is at his hungriest. This can help prevent a lot of stress at family meal times and avoids having an irritable, hungry child.

WHAT TIME'S TEA?

There's a lot to be said about the English system with tea at 5 pm and dinner later. We tend to gloss over the importance of tea (discussed here as the 4 o'clock binge), but a meal around this time is necessary. 'Tea' or dinner time is often later, especially if mum works. In some cases, particularly if your child has just started school, tea–dinner can be given after school when your child is hungriest, followed by a snack later on before bed. Children eat best when hungry, and this stops them filling up on junk foods rather than eating a nutritious meal.

Eating together at meal times

For many families eating meals together at the table is almost a thing of the past. This is a great pity because, not only did we learn about food and healthy eating, we learnt about good table manners, politics, current affairs and each person's daily activities. We discussed what we did at school and learnt about what our parents did at work. Eating together at the table is a time of social interaction and is a time of togetherness as a family.

Sadly many families eat in front of the television — obviously the favourite show is deemed to be more important than the family — or with the radio on, or if the family does eat at the table, the TV is also on.

In this day and age of video recorders, use them to record your favourite show if it is on at meal time, so that at least two to three times a week there is a family meal time without other distractions.

Because of family commitments it may not be possible to eat together until the weekend. It is a very special time for parents and you don't want to miss out on good family discussion nor the opportunity to provide information to your child. Of course this should have started when your child was a baby but it is not too late to start now.

Encourage your child to set the table — this can be fun, making the table look attractive, folding paper serviettes, even using pretty candles can create a restful and enjoyable atmosphere — and the kids love it!

Eating out and takeaways

his is always very exciting, particularly if eating out is a special occasion. Your child will feel very grown up about being allowed to choose what to eat. Many eat-in and takeaway outlets serve very high-fat, high-salt foods which are OK if your family eats out only once or twice a month, but if this type of eating out is more frequent, be selective about the type of venue that you and your family dine out at. Many restaurants and family food outlets have a range of healthy foods to choose from. Avoid fried foods most of the time.

As eating out is usually later than your child's usual meal time, offer a snack such as a piece of fruit, or crackers and cheese to take the edge of his appetite.

In some families there is the traditional 'fish and chips' every Friday night. This tradition can be improved upon by choosing grilled fish instead of the battered and deep-fried variety, eating less chips and adding a salad to the meal.

Here are some examples of how takeaway foods can be included in a healthy diet:

Chinese food – choose meat and vegetable dishes that are not fried.

Pizza – eat smaller serves of the meat varieties and include vegetarian varieties as well.

PUBS AND RESTAURANTS

Some hotels and restaurants offer children's meals with such gastronomical delights as fish and chips, hot dogs and chips, chicken and chips, tinned spaghetti and chips. This is followed by dessert of ice-cream and topping or ice-cream and hundreds and thousands.

At the same time parents dine on fillet steak, jacket potato and tossed salad or spaghetti marinara with desserts of fresh fruit salad, crackers, cheese and fruit.

Get the picture?

Caterers decide that your child would prefer fatty, salty food to tasty healthier food — so don't be in it, ask for a child's portion from the menu. Choose good food that is worth paying good money for. Why throw good money after bad! Interestingly enough, most children enjoy good food especially when eating out, particularly if it is well-presented in nice surroundings.

Rewards

Have you ever been guilty of rewarding your child with food? 'If you tidy your room, I'll buy you some chips for lunch.'

Rewards are given to children as a way of praising them for good behaviour or to say thank you. Many parents, well-meaning grandparents, friends and even teachers give foods such as lollies, chocolates, cakes, biscuits and chips as rewards. Most of these foods tend to be high in sugar and fat and low in nutritional value.

Food should definitely be enjoyed, but developing a habit of using it as a reward can bring on problems later in life. To avoid problems of tooth decay, overweight and obesity, try other tactics:

• An afternoon at the park on the play equipment.
• Visit a friend.
• Go to the cinema.
• Buy a book, puzzle, fancy pencils.
• Give swap-cards, balloons, a stamp on the hand, stickers.
• Contribute some money towards an article of 'trendy gear'.
• Go ice skating or roller skating.

Generally speaking, food rewards are not a good idea. Non-food rewards will be appreciated just as much or maybe even more!

Favourite Foods

Children like foods that are: familiar but interesting, such as Asian and Italian foods; don't like too many vegetables or salads with dressings; prefer finger foods; can't wait a long time for meals so you have to be quick; prefer small to medium serves; enjoy chicken drumsticks, satays, spaghetti, hamburgers, pizza, fish pieces and fish fingers, grated cheese, sandwiches, French bread with fillings, noodles; love ice-cream in a bowl, cone or on a stick!

CHAPTER SIX

Come On, You Must Be Hungry

Eat your dinner!

Fussy eating and food refusal

Y ou probably thought that by the time your child reached school age you'd be able to say goodbye to fussy eating. Not so! Between 5 and 12 years children are still likely to be fairly fussy, with very definite likes and dislikes. They usually have good appetites but, like the toddler, these vary during the day and from day to day. You'll know when they're going through a growth spurt — they'll eat extremely well. Don't forget that children at this age still have good appetite control so know when they're hungry and when they have had enough!

Recent research with parents indicated that the fussiest ages are between 3 and 9 years, and that only about one-third of children between 1 and 12 years will eat anything. The most disliked foods included vegetables (44%), fruit (16%), red meat (14%), fish (10%) and milk (5%), all foods which are nutritionally important. No wonder parents get worried!

So how do you handle the school-age child who supposedly won't eat or is fussy? Exactly the same way you handled your toddler. Remember two rules of thumb:

• A hungry child will eat.
• No healthy child has ever starved through food refusal.

Food refusal in school-age children, unlike that of the toddler, is not normally an attention seeking device to frustrate you. It occurs simply because the child has 'filled up' at other times of the day (such as after school) rather than at meal times or genuinely dislikes the food.

Unfortunately for parents, the hunger attacks of children usually occur outside traditional meal times!

And of course, on the flip side, after about 9 years your child will start to eat both snacks and meals!

TIPS FOR COPING

• Relax and make meals enjoyable, family occasions. Children eat better if they eat with others such as family or friends.

• If a child refuses to eat, remove the food calmly and let them leave the table. Do not allow any other food until the next scheduled meal. It's important to remember that children usually like foods they are not forced to eat.

• Serve small serves of food and let him ask for more.

• Keep your child active. This stimulates the appetite and is good for muscle toning and strength and preventing overweight.

• Avoid eating in front of the television.

• To encourage interest in food, let your child help with menu planning, shopping, preparation and cooking. Children at this age love to cook, and the measuring and weighing involved complement the mathematical skills they learn at school. Get them to read a cookbook and select some savoury recipes. Refer them to the recipes in Chapter Nine of this book.

• Encourage your child to eat savoury dishes rather than cakes and biscuits.

• Be prepared for the after-school snack attack.

It is the rare child that is not hungry after school. Make sure you have some sandwiches, fruit, raw vegetables, milk, cheese, yoghurt and savoury biscuits for your child at this time. Avoid serving cakes, chips, sweet biscuits and lollies which fill him up and have little nutritional value. Encourage your child to sit at the table with you for afternoon tea rather than eating on the run.

If you find your child is over hungry at this time, why not (if possible) serve him part of the dinner meal?

Some children are also very hungry because they don't eat their lunch. They have been too busy playing to eat. Find out if this is the case and ensure a 'little lunch' is ready when he comes home.

See Chapter Nine for recipes but some ideas for snacks include:

- Different breads with toppings, muffins, crumpets, bread sticks, scones, pikelets.
- Fruit buns, fruit breads, fruit muffins.
- Fresh, dried, snack pack fruits, fruit fingers, frozen fruit.
- Nuts, peanut butter on bread.
- Vegetable sticks — celery, carrot, zucchini.
- Baked beans or spaghetti on toast.
- Breakfast cereal.
- Yoghurt, milk puddings, custards, milk shakes, home-made milk ice-blocks.
- Instant noodles or leftover cooked pasta with grated cheese.
- Reduced-salt pretzels.
- Cheese cubes with crackers.

Some common problems and solutions

MY CHILD WILL NOT DRINK MILK

Milk is a very important source of calcium for bones and teeth. Adequate calcium intake throughout childhood and adolescence is important for the prevention of osteoporosis. Some children may not like plain milk but will take it flavoured, or as cheese, yoghurt, custards, or in white sauces. Add milk or cheese to vegetables and casseroles. If your child takes no dairy products he is unlikely to meet his calcium needs. Use a soy drink, flavoured or unflavoured that has added calcium — at least 120 mg of calcium per 100 ml (3½ fl oz) of milk — and use it in the same way as milk. While other foods such as salmon, sardines, some vegetables, fruits and nuts have calcium it is not in sufficient quantities to meet calcium requirements. If no dairy foods or calcium-fortified soy drinks are taken see your doctor or dietitian. A calcium supplement may be needed. (See Chapter Nine for ideas.)

MY CHILD WON'T EAT MEAT

Children are lazy chewers, and this seems to be a reason why meat, particularly red meat, is not eaten. Most will eat it as a hamburger, as mince (e.g. spaghetti bolognaise) or in a casserole. As with toddlers, meat must be moistened with gravy. Try it stir-fried with vegetables. Avoid overcooking grilled or roasted meats. Children love a chicken leg. Red meats (beef, lamb) are the best sources of iron, with smaller amounts being present in fish, chicken, pork. Try different minces. Lots of children like pâté, which is an excellent source of iron.

Protein and iron found in meat can also be found in breakfast cereals, bread, eggs, dairy foods, legumes such as baked beans, soy beans, kidney beans and ground nuts, for example peanut butter. (See Chapter Nine for ideas.)

MY CHILD WON'T EAT VEGETABLES

Many children will not eat cooked vegetables but will eat them raw. Salad vegetables are usually liked — cherry tomatoes, slices of cucumber, grated carrot or carrot sticks, celery, stringless beans, snow peas, squash, avocado. Serve them with a tasty dip. Raw vegetables are more manageable if they are slightly blanched.

While vegetables may not be eaten as a separate side dish they may be eaten if included (and perhaps disguised by grating) in meat loaf, rissoles, savoury mince and casseroles. Many children will eat vegetables if served as vegetable lasagne, in a stir-fry or in steamed or fried rice.

If no vegetables are eaten there is no need to panic, providing your child is eating fruit.

The same nutrients are found in vegetables as are in fruit. Make sure fruit is eaten cooked or raw not just as juice, which lacks fibre. Limit fruit juice and vegetable juice to 1–2 serves per day.

Keep offering vegetables in small quantities. In time you'll find he may accept them. Don't make a fuss. Relax and serve what he likes with occasional new ones to try. (See Chapter Nine for ideas on interesting vegetable recipes.)

MY CHILD EATS PEANUT BUTTER SANDWICHES EVERY DAY FOR LUNCH

There's no need to worry! Children are creatures of habit. Just as some adults eat the same for lunch every day, so do children. Peanut butter sandwiches are after all nutritious.

Despite elaborate recipe ideas for school lunches, you'll find most children are unadventurous and prefer spreads such as peanut butter, cheese spread, Vegemite or plain cheese. Fortunately, these are nutritious. Ask your child what he likes and vary these fillings. Provide variety by using different breads: white, mixed-grain, wholemeal, rye, rolls, pocket breads. (For recipe ideas, see Chapter Nine.)

Many children don't like salad vegetables on their sandwiches, as salad can make the bread soggy or else fall out and mess uniforms when the sandwich is being eaten.

Some children don't eat lunch, while other children swap their lunch with friends. A friend used to put notes, poems or drawings in her children's lunchbox to remind them to eat their lunch. Her children used to look forward to these surprise messages each day from mum!

MY CHILD WON'T EAT DINNER

Most likely because he has filled up on foods after school! Supervise after-school eating and limit quantities, so some appetite is left for the evening meal. If possible, serve part of the evening meal (e.g. main course or dessert) as the after-school snack.

If your child attends an after-school care centre or is looked after by other carers, enquire as to the snacks and drinks that have been eaten and the quantities.

MY CHILD WON'T EAT BREAKFAST

Breakfast is an important meal for children, and they should be encouraged to eat it. Studies have shown that children who don't eat breakfast have poorer memory and do not perform efficiently at school.

A recent survey of 5–12 year olds in Sydney found that 16% of children left home without breakfast. Breakfast does not need to be difficult — make it simple — a bowl of cereal, milk and juice. A study conducted in the USA showed that those children who ate ready-to-eat breakfast cereals not only at breakfast but at other times of the day (snacks, lunch, dinner) had a better intake of nutrients than those who didn't.

If your child does not like to eat at home in the morning prepare a sandwich with juice or fruit for him to eat on the way to school. This can be prepared the night before. Avoid letting him buy food on the way to school. Of the 20% of children in the Sydney survey who ate on the way to school, one-third ate confectionery — not a good way to start the day.

Talk to your child about why breakfast is important. Most school-age children are interested in their bodies and the importance of food to them.

Ideas for a quick breakfast to eat at home or on the run (see also Chapter Nine):
- Breakfast cereal with milk.
- Breakfast biscuits made into sandwiches with cheese, peanut butter or sliced banana.
- Sandwiches.
- Small packet of breakfast cereal eaten dry.
- Fruit juice and cheese and crackers.
- Fresh fruit and cold hard-boiled egg.
- Fruit bun.
- Carton of yoghurt.
- Eggnog or milk shake.
- Smoothie.

MY CHILD EATS TOO MANY JUNK FOODS

Ask yourself where the junk foods are coming from? Are they in the home, does he purchase them from the school canteen or the local shop with his pocket money, or does he get them from friends?

Occasional treats such as lollies, chocolates, cakes and biscuits are fine for children, but avoid having them in the house. If they are not available, your child will be less likely to ask for them and less likely to want them in preference to more nutritious foods. Remember, 'out of sight, is out of mind'.

Make sure canteen money for lunch is spent on a healthy lunch and not all on lollies. If your school canteen is not a 'healthy' one, talk to the school principal and the Parents & Friends Association and contact the School Canteen Association in your State.

Most children at primary school learn about their bodies and the importance of healthy eating. Many are proud and 'feel good' when they eat healthy foods. Give them lots of encouragement when they select a healthy food rather than a 'junk food'. Talk about the food and why it is good for them. Make sure that you also set a good example by always offering healthy choices.

My child only eats white bread

While your child may have eaten all types of bread as a pre-schooler, it appears that peer pressure influences what is eaten at school. Surveys show white bread is the preferred bread of school children. You shouldn't worry about this as, after all, white bread is nutritious and is much better than having no bread at all.

White bread contains protein, complex carbohydrate (starch), dietary fibre, vitamins and minerals, although the quantities (except for thiamine, as all bread has added thiamine), are lower than in wholemeal. However surveys show that white bread eaters actually eat more bread than wholemeal or mixed-grain eaters so some of the deficit in these nutrients is made up simply because more is eaten.

For extra fibre, use the white high-fibre loaves. To encourage the consumption of mixed-grain or wholemeal breads, make sandwiches with one slice of white and one slice of mixed-grain or wholemeal.

Vitamin and mineral supplements

Are they necessary?

Concern about poor diets and fussy eating has led some parents to supplement their children's diets with vitamins and minerals or seek the help of health professionals. One survey showed that nearly 50% of the parents with fussy eaters supplemented their children's diet with vitamins, 13% had thought about it, and 20% had sought advice from a health professional.

Generally, children do not need vitamin and mineral supplements and they are certainly no substitute for an adequate diet. It is better to offer your child a variety of foods he likes and to avoid supplements altogether unless he is sick or lifestyle circumstances demand them.

Before resorting to supplements, keep a food diary listing all the foods eaten over about 2–3 days and check these quantities with those recommended in the table 'Approximate Daily Food Intake for Children 5–12 Years' in Chapter Two. It's important to keep in mind that children will eat differently on different days and this is perfectly normal. If, after looking at the food diary and consulting that table, you still feel your child's diet is inadequate, a vitamin and mineral supplement may be necessary. Talk to your doctor or dietitian.

When selecting a supplement make sure it is labelled for children, as adult supplements are generally not suitable. Buy a reputable, well-known brand and make sure ingredients and quantities of nutrients are listed. Your pharmacist can advise you. It is best to buy a multivitamin supplement rather than one containing a single nutrient. This is because vitamins and minerals work together as a team and too much of one may affect the action of others and cause harm. Fat soluble vitamins such as vitamin A, D, E and K are stored in the body and are toxic at high doses. Iron supplements in excessive quantities are also dangerous, and taking iron supplements in excess of needs can have adverse effects on growth.

Remember, vitamin and mineral supplements and 'tonics' containing vitamins and minerals are not harmless substances. They should be kept out of reach of children and quantities given as directed. Children have been admitted to hospitals over the years because of overdosing on supplements.

In circumstances such as the following, supplements are needed:

- If your water supply is low in fluoride, a fluoride supplement may then be necessary (refer to Chapter Four).
- If your child is at nutritional risk because of a poor diet, anorexia or is eating a fad diet.
- If your child takes no dairy products or fortified soy drinks so his calcium intake is inadequate.
- If your child has a chronic disease such as cystic fibrosis.
- If your child consumes a strict vegetarian or vegan diet without adequate dairy or supplemented soy products, in which case vitamin B12, zinc, calcium and iron may be needed.

Jam sandwiches for lunch?

While not the most nutritionally ideal filling on a sandwich, if taken occasionally, jam will do no harm. Jam on bread is a vehicle for getting children to eat bread, a nutritious source of protein, starch, fibre and vitamins and minerals. Often it may be a choice of jam sandwiches or no lunch at all. As lunch is important, we'd opt for the jam sandwich!

CHAPTER SEVEN

KIDS WITH SPECIAL DIETARY NEEDS

Helpful hints on coping

If your child is on a special diet

It would be remiss of us as dietitians not to give parents some helpful hints on coping with kids on special diets. You may have a child with allergies, diabetes, cystic fibrosis, coeliac disease or one of a number of conditions where diet is an important part of treatment. It is important to regularly attend your child's dietitian, as many things change and often diets become much easier to manage as more information about some conditions is being discovered. Where possible, the whole family should eat the same food as the child. Before going on an outing, discuss with your child what foods are OK and what should be avoided. In extreme cases it may be necessary for your child to eat before going out and/or take food with

him. Where possible, however, make sure your child understands everything about his diet and teach him how to make the right choices.

SCHOOL OUTINGS

Excursions
Provide your child with food for snacks and lunch as well as some drink. Discuss with the teacher beforehand what the key issues about your child's diet are.

School camps
These are always a cause for worry when a special diet is needed. Unfortunately the food at many school camps is far from suitable for active, growing children and can often include foods such as sausages, chips and desserts, and if vegetables are served, they are usually cooked to a tasteless pulp! A child should be

encouraged to attend camp and put theory into practice. It is also a good test of independence, after all, help is only a telephone call away.

Again, discuss the key issues with the attending teacher and contact the camp organisation to obtain a copy of the menu. Discuss suitable meal alternatives where necessary. Provide your child with extra food; for example, a child with coeliac disease cannot eat a hot dog in a roll, but meat and salad would be easy to prepare as an alternative. Usually the special diet alternative is healthier than the menu item, so you can even do the camp proprietors a favour by suggesting that all the children eat the healthier alternative!

As your child grows up, allow him to take over the responsibility of making healthy choices — you don't want him tied to your apron strings forever!

Common ailments

CONSTIPATION

Some children complain about a 'tummy ache' and while there are many reasons (such as anxiety or illness) constipation is quite a common and distressing problem in children but it can easily be fixed! Children need a high-fibre diet including fruits, vegetables, breads and cereals. Dried fruit such as prunes have special laxative effects and can easily be included in the daily diet. Children who miss breakfast miss an opportunity to eat some high-fibre food. Check Chapter Nine for high-fibre recipes. Constipation is a

distressing condition and is best avoided. See 'A to Z' (page 99).

DIARRHOEA

Aside from infection, diarrhoea can also be caused by anxiety and can be treated with a high-fibre diet. Strange as it may seem, chronic diarrhoea with no known cause can often respond to more fibre in the diet which 'bulks up' the 'poos'. An excess of fruit juice can aggravate diarrhoea. Reduce the fruit juice and increase the fruits, vegetables, bread and cereals in the diet and the problem is often quickly fixed. For persistent diarrhoea take your child to the doctor. See 'A to Z' (page 101).

'TUMMY ACHES'

These can occur in children for a range of real or perceived problems. If your child persists in having these ailments it may be necessary to consult your family doctor and your child's teacher. Don't dismiss anxieties in your child, address the situation now and prevent problems later.

END-OF-TERM SNIFFLES

Many children become run down towards the end of each term and seem to be more susceptible to colds, flu and throat infections. Considering that children spend a lot of time in close proximity to each other this is not surprising. In the earlier years of school, children do become tired, but if they are unwell, a day or two at home can help them recover quickly and prevent spreading germs to other children.

MUMPS, CHICKEN POX AND MEASLES

These are also common during early school years and are another reason to keep your child at home if unwell, in case he has one of these ailments. With the immunisation of babies, these conditions can usually be largely prevented. Don't dismiss any of these childhood conditions lightly — get an appropriate diagnosis and keep your child at home as long as necessary.

Nourishing diets for sick children

FLUIDS

Plenty of fluids are essential, particularly if your child has a fever. Try cold fluids, such as one of the following:

- Lemonade (not the low-joule variety)
- Milk shakes, smoothies, eggflips, Sustagen
- Fruit juices
- Sports drinks (e.g. Lucozade)
- Plus extra water

Ice to suck or fruit juice frozen into ice-blocks are usually appreciated. Keep a glass of water beside the bed and encourage the child to sip frequently.

'LIGHT' FOODS

Food is important to provide essential nutrients which are necessary to help fight infection.

Suitable light foods include the following:

- Yoghurt
- Ice-cream
- Small sandwiches
- Crackers with cheese
- Milk puddings such as custard, rice custard, blancmange, stewed or canned fruit
- Soups
- Bread

Offer snacks, frequent meals and drinks.

Milk and mucus

Does milk cause mucus?

Not in healthy people. Although milk is often restricted in children's diets because parents believe it causes mucus (i.e. coughs and congestion), scientific research has not shown any link between milk and mucus production in healthy people and it appears unrelated to colds or flu.

However, cow's milk has been shown to produce a small increase in congestion in some asthmatic children, probably as a result of a mild undiagnosed cow's milk intolerance. Restriction of cow's milk limits important nutrients such as calcium that growing children need. If cow's milk is restricted, substitute with a calcium-fortified soy beverage.

CHAPTER EIGHT

FUN FOOD ACTIVITIES

How to beat the boredom blues!

Games, crafts and hours of fun

When you've blown your budget and the kids are whingeing that there's nothing to do on weekends or during school holidays, try some of the fun food activities below to 'spark' their interest.

WHAT'S FOR DINNER?

Dinner party

Get the children to plan, shop and prepare a meal for the family or for their friends. Select a meal occasion (breakfast, lunch or dinner), date and time.

The meal may have a theme such as Asian, curry, Italian, Mexican, Easter, Christmas, party.

Encourage them to look through your recipe books to select recipes or use some of the simple recipes in Chapter Nine of this book.

Ask the children to write down the menu and prepare a shopping list. Make a time

when you take them shopping. Get them to look for the food items and, when necessary, weigh quantities.

Talk to them about basic hygiene and safety in the kitchen. You'll need to help them with basic cooking skills and supervise cooking. Children as young as 5 love to chop, grate, mix, stir, add spices.

Let them set the table, serve guests and family members (with help for younger children), and don't forget that they should clean up afterwards.

A BEAUTIFUL TABLE

Table craft

Make a centrepiece for the table. Some ideas include:

• Fresh flowers or other plants from the garden can be put in a pretty vase or pot.

• Egg-carton flowers can be made by cutting egg-carton sections separately and getting children to paint and decorate them. Make a hole in the centre of the egg-carton section and push a pipe cleaner through the hole for the stem. Double the pipe cleaner in the hole to stop the flower from falling. Real leaves or coloured paper leaves can be pasted onto the pipe cleaner to give an extra effect. Put the 'flowers' in a decorated paper cup.

- Tissue-paper flowers can also create a good effect. Crumple small coloured squares of tissue paper and paste onto twigs or branches collected from the garden. Fill a decorated margarine container with soil or sand and stand the flowers in it. Add some real 'greenery' from the garden to give more effect.
- Make a decorated tree. Set a tall branch or a shrub in a decorated plastic container filled with sand. Hang jewellery, small ornaments, home-made decorations or plastic fruits and vegetables from its branches.

Decorate a paper tablecloth
Ask children to decorate a plain paper tablecloth with drawings, pictures etc. A roll of paper tablecloth is ideal for this, but you could join large sheets of butcher's or other plain paper to fit table.

GAMES

Play 'What am I?'
One child describes a food he likes to eat that is 'good for you', while his friends guess what it is. The child who guesses it correctly has the next turn.

Example: I am long, curved, yellow and easy to peel — what am I?

A banana.

MAKE SANDWICHES, CAKES AND BISCUITS

Make sandwich faces for lunch or a snack
Thinly spread butter or margarine on a slice of white or wholemeal bread. Cover with grated cheese. Sprinkle with grated carrot for hair, use two large raisins or sultanas for the eyes, a celery stick for the nose and a thin wedge of red apple (leave skin) for the mouth.

Have an afternoon tea party with friends
Children can bake some cakes, biscuits and make small sandwiches and drinks (see Chapter Nine).

Bake some cakes or biscuits for grandparents or an elderly neighbour
Give the biscuits in a decorated container (such as an ice-cream or margarine container) with a home-made card.

FUN CRAFT PROJECTS

Make your own recipe book
Decorate the cover of an exercise book with food pictures and call it *My Recipe Book*. Record in it the recipes for favourite foods. Write down the recipes of any foods you cook.

Make a colourful poster of 'Foods I Like'
Cut out food pictures from magazines and glue on a large sheet of paper or cardboard.

Make a food mobile

Cut out food pictures from magazines and paste on both sides of cardboard. Punch a hole at the top of the pictures and thread through string or wool. Hang pictures from a decorated wire coat hanger.

Make a collage using food

Macaroni, spaghetti, fruit seeds, dried peas, beans, nuts, are excellent to paint and paste on paper.

Make your own photograph album

Collect old and recent photographs of your child to show how he has grown and changed. Put them in a special album you have made or bought. Your child can write a story about his life from the photos.

Make a healthy eating poster

On one half of the poster, paste pictures of foods that are good for you and on the other side paste foods that are not so good for you.

FOOD TO GROW

Create a vegetable patch

Select a patch of ground in the garden (or use a planter tray) and plant some vegetable seeds. Beans, radish, corn, parsley and mint grow quickly. Water the seeds and watch them grow.

Sprout some mung beans for sandwiches

Put some mung beans in a large jar with water. Soak overnight, then drain off water and place in a dark, dry, warm cupboard. Rinse with cool water twice per day. Look at changes daily — changes in colour, size, hardness. Sprouts are ready in a few days. Use on sandwiches or in salads.

STORIES AND MUSIC

Story

Write a story about the foods I like and why they make me healthy.

Make an orchestra with musical shakers made using food

Put rice in an empty milk or juice bottle. Screw on lid.

Put dried beans in a can. Replace lid.

Put macaroni in a toilet-paper roll. Seal with foil at both ends and decorate.

SHAPES AND HEIGHTS

What do I look like?

On a large piece of paper get your child and his friends to draw a full-size outline of themselves. Let them colour and mark in details of parts of their bodies (face, hands etc.). Children can see how each of them is different and special with regard to shape and height. Children may like to paste pictures of foods that help them grow.

How tall am I?

Using a long thin strip of paper 85 cm (34 in) in length and 8 cm (3 in) in width, mark heights in 5 cm (2 in) sections beginning with the base marked 80 cm (32 in), up to the top at 165 cm (66 in). Children can decorate the strip of paper. Place chart on wall 80 cm (32 in) from the floor. Children will have fun marking their heights and watching how they grow.

MORE FOOD FUN

Make your own bread

Use a bread mix or a recipe from your favourite recipe book. Eat it fresh and warm straight from the oven!

Turn milk into yoghurt

You'll need 4 tablespoons of commercial plain yoghurt and 600 ml (1 pt) of milk. In a saucepan, heat the milk until it is warm, but not boiling (71°C/190°F). Pour into a glass bowl that takes at least 600 ml (1 pt). Cool until it is lukewarm (43°C/110°F). Add yoghurt, which should be at room temperature. Stir until well blended. Cover with a towel to keep warm. Let stand at room temperature for at least 8–12 hours. When ready the yoghurt will move away from the sides of the container. Place in fridge. Taste it plain, then try it with fresh fruit. Home-made yoghurt won't be as thick as commercial yoghurt.

Turn grapes into sultanas

Buy fresh, ripe, seedless grapes. Wash thoroughly. Dry well with paper towel. Spread a layer of grapes on a tray. Cover with clean tea towel or other cloth and fasten so it will not blow away. Place on blocks to dry, away from dirt so air can circulate over and under tray. After about 4 days test grapes for dryness by squeezing them. If there is no moisture on your hand and they spring apart when hand is opened they are ready. Look at the difference in colour, texture, taste between fresh grapes and dried. Eat the sultanas as a snack.

Make your own peanut butter

You'll need peanuts roasted in their shells and some oil.

Remove peanuts from shell. Put one cup of peanuts and 1½ tablespoons of oil in a blender. Blend till you get a smooth texture. Add salt if required. Spread on bread, crackers or celery.

A SPECIAL OUTING

Visit a food factory, a farm, an orchard

Visit a place where food comes from and look for books and videos about how food is grown and processed.

Nutrition in a can

Do canned foods have much nutritional value?

Canned foods offer variety and are quick and convenient to use. Recent research undertaken by the Australian Government Analytical Laboratories into the nutritional value of a range of canned fruits, vegetables, soups and complete meals have shown they have similar nutritional value to foods freshly prepared in the home.

CHAPTER NINE

FOOD AND RECIPE IDEAS FOR HEALTHY KIDS

Easy, nutritious meals and snacks

Buying and preparing food

HEALTHY SHOPPING HABITS

Kids love to go shopping. There is always a chance that mum or dad might be 'whinged' into buying the latest food advertised on the telly that 'everyone' has. As mentioned under Chapter Five, kids are very influenced by TV advertising so be aware of that fact. Peer pressure also starts to raise its ugly head and you may be fascinated to know that your child probably has the 'meanest mother' in the world, particularly if you don't buy the latest 'in' food.

Kids can be a great help when shopping nevertheless. Always write a list *before* you leave home. Manufacturers of sweets and snack food lines rely on 'impulse' buying, and you will notice that these items are always placed near the checkout. Some supermarkets provide small shopping trolleys for kids. Ask your child to collect five items that are on your list. For older children who can read, give them part of your list to fill. Remember, a shopping list puts you in control and is essential if you are to stick to your family food budget and bring home essentials rather than junk foods. The alternative to taking your kids with you is to shop alone — this is an excellent way to save money!

KITCHEN HYGIENE AND SAFETY

It goes without saying that when preparing and cooking food, hygiene is important. Bacteria are present in our bodies, in our kitchens, in the refrigerator, everywhere. Some bacteria are harmless but others cause food spoilage which can cause illness and even death. Clean food habits reduce the chance of food poisoning. Did you know that the most common causes of food related illness occur in our own kitchens? So what can we do to prevent it happening? We want our children to be healthy and, importantly, not to miss any school. Encourage your kids to help in the kitchen but also make sure that you teach these rules for cleanliness as well.

- Wash your hands before handling food and *before eating*.
- Keep the kitchen utensils clean, and clean up as you go. Apart from saving time cleaning up, it reduces the chance of germs in the kitchen.
- If you are using a wooden chopping board, scrub it under running hot water after use. Some scientists think that a plastic board is safer to use. In either case, the message is to scrub the board under running hot water after use.
- Wear a clean apron when preparing food. Your family needs to be protected from your clothes. Tie up your long hair — who needs hair in their stew?
- Buy good quality fruit and vegetables. Buy only enough for a few days.
- If in doubt throw it out. Most leftovers can be stored in the refrigerator for up to 48 hours.
- Always refrigerate prepared foods in covered containers.

- Don't leave food sitting around on the kitchen bench to cool. Place food in a shallow container, then place the container in cold water to cool it as quickly as possible before putting it in the fridge.
- Defrost meat by placing in the fridge for 24 hours.
- When reheating food from the refrigerator, bring to boiling point then cool before serving. Even in the fridge, bacteria produce spores which can cause sickness, however most of these are destroyed by boiling.

COOKING MADE EASY — USING CONVENIENCE ITEMS

As well as fresh food there is available a range of foods that are dried, canned or frozen. There is also the convenience of foods that are already part of a meal and only require something to be added. Foods such as sauces for casseroles and packet cakes are part of our daily diet and help busy parents to prepare quick easy meals. Canned and frozen fruits and vegetables are easy to use, add variety to our diets and are nutritious. On the other hand frozen meals and desserts may not be items which necessarily suit your family's healthy diet. Include these occasionally for a change.

Use some of these foods to add more variety and for convenience: frozen fruits and vegetables, canned vegetables (choose reduced-salt varieties), canned fruit (choose fruit in light syrup or water), dried vegetables (these are not as popular these days, as most people have a freezer or choose fresh or canned varieties).

If you are a busy parent trying to juggle parenthood with work, take advantage of many of the convenience foods available which are usually just as nutritious as the fresh item and sometimes are even better, as fresh foods start to deteriorate as soon as they are picked. Let's face it, a carrot in your refrigerator after a week is not worth eating but a frozen carrot in your freezer after a month is almost as nutritious as the day it was frozen, which is only a matter of hours after being picked.

HELPFUL HINTS FOR WORKING PARENTS

At the end of a busy day the last thing you want to do is get a meal prepared. The kids are tired and scratchy, there is homework to help with, baths to see to, a load of washing to do and probably some clothes to iron for tomorrow. Hungry people cope better when fed, including you!

Imagine this — you walk in the door, and within 15 minutes the family is sitting down to eat. Afterwards every one feels relaxed and sets about the evening chores. Impossible you say?

We are working mums and as the saying goes have 'been there, done that'. The solution is simple. Work every day in advance. Cook tomorrow's meal tonight, even up to plating it up and placing in the refrigerator. As soon as you walk in the door each evening, simply place each meal in the microwave for a couple of minutes and you can start the evening off together in a relaxed manner. Once the meal is over, prepare and cook the next evening's meal. Casseroles, roasts, grills, stir-frys, pasta and rice dishes all reheat in the microwave very successfully. Taking the pressure off at meal time is an important part of coping with a busy lifestyle.

Life without a microwave

Even without a microwave you can still reheat meals successfully. The easiest way is not to plate out the meals, but to reheat in the cooking utensil (except for roasts and grills, which can be wrapped in foil and reheated in the oven).

Quick meals for healthy kids

The easiest way to put good nutrition into practice is to use healthy recipes. Our recipes have been developed for the whole family and are prepared without added salt and with minimal amounts of sugar and fat. Reduced-fat milk and dairy products have been used in all recipes requiring milk; however, you may prefer to use regular milk.

- To grease pans use ½ teaspoon of vegetable oil and use a pastry brush to spread it around.
- Use cast-iron pans for cooking, as they heat quickly and only small amounts of oil are required to cook the food.
- Use your microwave oven to cook foods wherever possible rather than to only reheat food. This will save you valuable time and money.

Beaut breakfasts

Remember how important breakfast is for school children. Refer to Chapter Five for important information on breakfast.

Breakfast for 'Non-breakfast' Breakfast Eaters

Quick Morning Pick-me-up

PREPARATION TIME: 2 MINUTES

½ cup (125 ml/4 fl oz) milk
Fruit (e.g. ½ banana, ½ dozen fresh
strawberries)
1 tablespoon fruit yoghurt

Blend together.
Serve in a tall glass with a straw.
Delicious!

SERVES 1

~

Hot Choco Orange

PREPARATION TIME: 2 MINUTES

½ cup (125 ml/4 fl oz) reduced-fat milk
1 teaspoon Aktavite or Milo
½ teaspoon grated orange rind

Stir together, heat in the microwave 10
seconds (check the temperature as there
are variations in microwave energy levels).
Stir before serving.

SERVES 1

~

Yoghurt with Fruit

PREPARATION TIME: 1 MINUTE

2 tablespoons yoghurt (fruit or plain)
Chopped fresh fruit such as ½ chopped apple,
mandarin, strawberries, cantaloupe

Mix together and serve.

SERVES 1

Breakfast for Breakfast Eaters

Cereal is a good breakfast food to start the day. Take care to choose healthy breakfast cereals as some are high in added sugar and fat. Wholegrain cereals are the best choices as well as old favourites such as porridge, and biscuit style cereals. You may wish to make your own cereals. Ingredients are readily available in the supermarket and allow you more variety.

Porridge is easy to prepare, just 1–2 minutes in the microwave, and is often enjoyed by children. Use milk rather than water for a creamier taste.

Yummy Cereal

PREPARATION TIME: 5 MINUTES

4 cups wheat flakes
1 teaspoon cinnamon
½ cup sultanas
½ cup chopped dried apricots
½ cup wheatgerm

Mix together. Store in an airtight
container.
Serve with milk, yoghurt or fruit juice.

SERVES 4–6

~

OTHER BREAKFAST IDEAS

- Baked beans on toast — choose salt-reduced varieties.
- Eggs — a great protein source and easy to prepare. Serve boiled with fingers of toast, scrambled or poached.
- Sandwiches are another nutritious food for breakfast as well as lunch. Serve toasted for a change.
- Fruit, either fresh or canned, is a good start to the day. Add yoghurt or custard.

CINNAMON TOAST

PREPARATION TIME: 2 MINUTES

2 slices of white or wholemeal bread
1 tablespoon ricotta cheese
½ teaspoon sugar
½ teaspoon cinnamon

Toast bread, spread with ricotta then sprinkle lightly with sugar and cinnamon. Cut into fingers.

SERVES 1

~

Time for lunch

LUNCHBOX IDEAS — ORDINARY SANDWICHES MADE SPECIAL

Some children eat peanut butter or jam sandwiches 'ad infinitum' and point blank refuse to eat anything else. Fortunately, in time, they become more adventurous and become willing to try new flavours.

Hints for healthy and enjoyable sandwiches include:

- Reduce unnecessary fat by using our fat-free recipe for mayonnaise (Easy Mayonnaise, page 78), instead of butter or margarine.
- White bread is very nutritious, so if your child does not enjoy wholemeal varieties, white bread is OK — particularly as there are many white 'high-fibre' varieties on the market.
- Use lean cooked meat in preference to 'sausage varieties', although of course that can be used for the dog!
- Pack pieces of chopped or grated vegetables so that your child can either eat them separately or add to his or her sandwich.
- Don't add salt to sandwiches, choose reduced-salt sauces and spreads and use sparingly.
- Tomato tends to make sandwiches soggy.
- 'Soggy' sandwiches are a big 'no no' so avoid foods such as wet lettuce, tomatoes, 'wet' beetroot — this needs to be well drained.
- Some fillings (eggs, fish of any kind, garlic meats) are rather smelly and not popular with other students when the lid of the lunchbox is removed! These foods are best eaten when sandwiches are freshly made.
- Try different bases for sandwiches such as pocket bread or rice cakes for a change. With the prospect of 12 or so years of school with sandwiches every day, a change is welcome!

See if you can tempt your child with these fillings:

- Reduced-fat cream cheese mixed with finely chopped celery and sultanas.
- Grated carrot and cheese with a teaspoon of Easy Mayonnaise (page 78).
- Mashed avocado, Easy Mayonnaise and chopped cooked chicken.
- Finely chopped celery, apple and Easy Mayonnaise, add grated cheese and pile into pocket bread.
- Leftover roast meat with grated carrot, chopped lettuce and chutney (or tomato sauce).
- Cheese, pineapple ring (well drained and patted dry) with lean ham.
- A lightly buttered roll and a banana to be put together at lunch time (instead of a banana sandwich).

LUNCHBOX TREATS — TRY A CHANGE FROM SANDWICHES

These easy to prepare and tasty finger foods are ideal for the lunchbox.

To keep your child's lunch cool, place a small ice brick in the lunchbox. As well as keeping the food cool and fresh it is more hygienic as it reduces bacterial growth. Remember that bacteria love warm conditions.

TASTY CHICKEN DRUMSTICKS

PREPARATION TIME: 10 MINUTES
FREEZING: SUITABLE

6 chicken drumsticks
2 tablespoons salt-reduced soy sauce
1 tablespoon water
1 tablespoon apricot jam
1 clove garlic, crushed

Remove skin from drumsticks, combine the remaining ingredients and marinate the chicken for at least 2 hours.
Preheat oven to 200°C (400°F). Bake drumsticks in the oven on a lightly greased tray for 45 minutes. Cool for a few minutes and then store in a covered container in the refrigerator.
Hint: Prepare a dozen drumsticks at a time, freeze singly and remove the required number the night before to defrost in the fridge.

SERVES 6 SMALL CHILDREN OR 3 HUNGRY ONES!

~

CHICKEN MEATBALLS

PREPARATION TIME: 15 MINUTES
FREEZING: SUITABLE

500 g (1 lb) lean chicken mince (specialty chicken shops have good quality mince)
3 spring onions (green onions), finely chopped
6 sprigs parsley, finely chopped
1 small carrot, grated
1 teaspoon prepared French mustard (not the hot variety)
2 tablespoons plain flour
1 egg

Preheat oven to 200°C (400°F). Combine ingredients. Roll walnut sized pieces into balls and place on a lightly greased baking tray. Bake for 15 minutes. Turn meatballs over and bake for a further 10 minutes. Cool on greaseproof paper.

MAKES 16 MEATBALLS

VARIATIONS

Teriyaki Meatballs: Substitute minced beef for chicken and use soy sauce in place of French mustard.
Sweet and Sour Meatballs: Substitute lean pork mince for chicken, add 1 tablespoon soy sauce and 1 tablespoon drained crushed pineapple.

~

VEGIE BALLS

PREPARATION TIME: 20 MINUTES
FREEZING: SUITABLE

2 cups cooked mashed pumpkin
4 chopped spring onions (green onions)
½ cup cooked and mashed parsnip
½ cup chopped parsley
2 tablespoons plain flour
2 teaspoons oyster sauce
sesame seeds

Preheat oven to 220°C (425°F). Mix all ingredients except sesame seeds, shape into 8 small patties and roll in sesame seeds. Press seeds lightly into the patties with fingers. Place on a lightly greased tray and bake for 10–15 minutes.

SERVES 4

~

TURKEY ROLLS

PREPARATION TIME: 10 MINUTES
FREEZING: NOT SUITABLE

turkey breast (this is available at good delicatessens) — allow 4 thin slices turkey breast per child
cranberry sauce
Easy Potato Salad (page 77) — allow 1 teaspoon per slice of turkey

Spread cranberry sauce on turkey breast, place potato salad in the centre. Roll up. Keep chilled in refrigerator until ready to go to school. It is not a good idea to serve this on a very hot day.

~

VEGETABLE SLICE

PREPARATION TIME: 30 MINUTES
FREEZING: SUITABLE

This dish is suitable hot or cold as a weekend meal or main meal. It is delicious cold, and you may find that kids who are not so keen on vegies really enjoy this.

2 large zucchinis
2 large carrots
1 large onion
½ cup grated cheese
220 g sweet corn kernels
4 eggs
2 rashers of lean bacon, finely chopped
1 cup (125 g/4 oz) self-raising flour

Preheat oven to 200°C (400°F).
Coarsely grate the zucchini, carrots and
onions (you can use a food processor).
Combine all the ingredients and press into
a lightly greased lasagne dish.
Bake for 1 hour.

SERVES 6 FOR A MEAL (OR CUT INTO SMALLER
SQUARES WHEN COLD
AS AN INTERESTING SCHOOL LUNCH)
SERVES 4

~

TUNA AND RICE SLICE

PREPARATION TIME: 20 MINUTES
FREEZING: SUITABLE

½ cup rice
1 × 425 g (13 oz) can tuna in spring water,
drained
4–6 spring onions (green onions), chopped
220 g (7 oz) sweet corn kernels
½ cup chopped celery
2 eggs

Cook rice. While rice is cooking, preheat
oven to 200°C (400°F).
Drain the rice well, then combine with
other ingredients. Put mixture in a
lamington tin. Bake for 20 minutes.
Cut into squares when cold.

SERVES 4

~

CHICKEN AND PASTA SALAD

PREPARATION TIME: 10 MINUTES
FREEZING: NOT SUITABLE

Any kind of leftovers are popular for
lunch, such as:
- Quiche
- Chicken
- Rissoles
- Salad
- Vegetables

This is an interesting way to use up
leftovers. In a small plastic bowl (with lid)
place chopped cooked chicken, cooked
pasta, leftover cooked vegetables, or diced
raw tomato and spring onion (green
onion) finely chopped, add 1 tablespoon
Easy Mayonnaise (page 78). Combine.
Don't forget to pack a fork and serviette.

~

BREAD CASES

PREPARATION TIME: 20 MINUTES
FREEZING: SUITABLE (UNFILLED)

Try filling these bread cases with leftovers
for a nice change.

12 slices of bread
1 egg
1 tablespoon milk

Preheat oven to 220°C (425°F).
Flatten each slice of bread with a rolling
pin. Using a biscuit cutter or large tea cup,
cut out the middle of the bread. Beat egg
and milk together and brush lightly over
bread rounds. Press into lightly greased
patty tins. Bake for 10 minutes. Bake until
crisp and golden. Allow to cool then fill.
Suggested fillings include: anything in
white sauce such as chicken, tuna, canned
creamed corn, canned mushrooms;
leftover stew.

HOT LUNCHES

On cold days you may be close enough to be able to take your child a hot lunch — try soup, toasted sandwiches or hot leftovers such as last night's casserole. Older children can take hot foods to school in an insulated container, but little children can easily get burnt so this is not a safe practice.

THE SCHOOL CANTEEN

Some days you may want your child to buy his lunch and kids enjoy choosing for themselves. Unfortunately not all canteens provide healthy choices of food and while it's OK for your child to sometimes have 'junk food', if your child buys his lunch frequently, say, two to three times a week, and chooses 'junk food' then his diet is not going to be very healthy.

Good canteen choices include:
- Sandwiches
- Rolls
- Steamed dim sims
- Salads
- Fresh fruit
- Vegetables
- Milk drinks (reduced-fat varieties)
- Yoghurt (reduced-fat varieties)
- Bottled water
- Low-joule drinks
- Fruit juice
- Plain ice-cream (avoid chocolate coated varieties)
- Plain popcorn

Bad canteen choices include:
- Pies (OK occasionally but don't be fooled by wholemeal pastry — it's the fat in the pastry that is the health hazard — there is nothing magical about wholemeal pastry)
- Pasties (ditto)
- Sausages
- Any fried foods such as potato cakes, chips, chicken nuggets
- Hot dogs
- Lollies
- Carob bars
- Chocolate bars
- Muesli bars
- Icy poles
- Chocolate coated biscuits and cream cakes – these are too high in fat
- Soft drinks
- Chocolate coated ice-creams
- Packet crisps and other packet snack foods

Generally speaking it is easier to provide healthier food from home.

Snacks and light meals

THE FOUR O'CLOCK SNACK ATTACK

Most children are starving when they arrive home from school. Often they have been too busy at school to eat, and it is not unusual for children to bring some or all of their lunch home (particularly the little ones). Four o'clock can be time for a substantial meal or some snack food. Don't allow your child to fill up on 'junk' while he waits for his evening meal. For younger children, if possible, a good meal is best served at this time as often they are too tired to eat at the family meal time. Later a light snack or part of the meal can be enjoyed when dad and or mum return home from work.

Light meal ideas

- Grilled cheese on toast
- Toasted sandwiches
- Baked beans on toast or as a filling for the sandwich maker
- Yoghurt
- Fresh fruit
- Pop an apple into the microwave (don't forget to make cuts in the skin) for 5 minutes, sprinkle with cinnamon and serve with yoghurt
- Muffins (see recipe page 82)
- Crackers with cheese and tomato
- Soup

Meal ideas

- Leftovers
- Serve the meal of the day and provide fruit and yoghurt later on
- Soup (there's nothing like a thick vegetable soup on a cold day)
- Jacket potatoes
- Cooked pasta with ready-to-serve sauces (there are endless varieties on the market)

Choose from one of our recipes. They are suitable for all the family.

Snack Foods

Children generally prefer, and in fact need, food often throughout the day so snack foods must be chosen carefully. Too often kids fill up on 'junk food' leaving little room for healthy foods and consequently pay the price — poor school performance, illness, lack of energy, irritability. The following foods are quick and easy energy boosters:

- Plain popcorn (don't add anything)
- Fresh fruit
- Canned fruit, fruit snack packs
- Crackers and cheese
- Yoghurt
- Sandwiches
- Slices of toast
- Bread sticks
- Home-made recipe from our 'Fillers' section (page 82).

Easy dinners

At the end of a busy day, no-one wants to spend hours in the kitchen preparing food. Most meals in this section can be on the table within half an hour of starting preparation.

Prepare tomorrow night's dinner tonight (after everyone has eaten) plate it up, cover, refrigerate, then microwave to reheat. If you haven't got a microwave, skip the plating bit, reheat the food conventionally then serve.

SOUP

A hearty soup is a meal in itself and is great at weekends with crusty bread or as a snack after school. Some children even enjoy soup for breakfast!

HEALTHY VEGETABLE SOUP

PREPARATION TIME: 10 MINUTES
FREEZING: SUITABLE

1 onion
2 large potatoes
2 large carrots
1 medium parsnip
1 × 440 g (14 oz) can tomatoes
4 salt-reduced chicken stock cubes
1 litre (32 fl oz) water
1 teaspoon oil
½ cup (80 g/3 oz) noodles

Chop up vegetables. Heat oil in a large saucepan . Add chopped vegetables, brown and then add tomatoes, crumbled stock cubes, water. Simmer 40 minutes until vegetables are tender. Add noodles. Cook a further 15 minutes.

SERVES 6

PUMPKIN SOUP

PREPARATION TIME: 10 MINUTES
FREEZING: SUITABLE

1 small pumpkin
2 onions
1 teaspoon oil
6 salt-reduced chicken stock cubes
1 cup (250 ml/8 fl oz) water
2 cups (500 ml/16 fl oz) milk
2–3 spring onions (green onions), chopped
black pepper (optional)

Peel pumpkin and chop into chunks. Peel onions and chop roughly. Heat oil in a large saucepan. Add vegetables and stir quickly. Add crushed chicken cubes and water. Place lid on saucepan and simmer for 1 hour. Turn heat off and cool. Blend soup in a mouli or processor until smooth. Return to saucepan, add milk, black pepper (if using) and chopped spring onions (green onions). This makes a big pot. If you are lucky and the family doesn't go back for seconds, you can freeze the leftovers.

SERVES 6

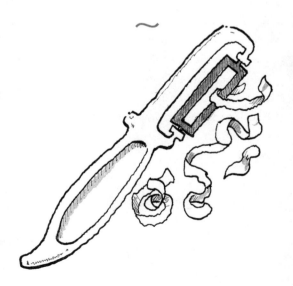

Sarah's Favourite Chicken and Sweet Corn Soup

PREPARATION TIME: 5 MINUTES
FREEZING: NOT SUITABLE

1 packet salt-reduced chicken noodle soup
1 × 440 g (14 oz) can creamed sweet corn
1 egg

Make up packet soup according to directions but using only three-quarters of the water. Cook soup for the required time, add can of creamed corn (undrained). Beat egg and pour into the boiling soup in a thin stream, stirring quickly.
Serve with crusty bread or as a snack after school.

SERVES 6

~

Beef and lamb

Easy Stroganoff Casserole

PREPARATION TIME: 10 MINUTES
FREEZING: SUITABLE

1 onion
1 green capsicum (pepper)
1 large carrot
500 g (1 lb) stir-fry beef (buy it already cut at the supermarket)
1 packet salt-reduced mushroom soup
1 cup water

Preheat oven to 200°C (400°F).
Cut vegetables into thin strips. Place meat and vegetables into a casserole dish.
Sprinkle soup over the top then add water.
Cover and cook in oven for 1½ hours, stirring from time to time.
Serve with rice and tossed salad.

SERVES 4

Easy Stir-fry

PREPARATION TIME: 30 MINUTES
FREEZING: CAN FREEZE BUT WILL BE A LITTLE 'SOGGY'

500 g (1 lb) stir-fry beef (buy it already cut at the supermarket)
1 onion, diced
1 green capsicum (pepper), cut into strips
½ cup frozen beans
2 carrots, cut into thin strips
1 head broccoli cut into flowerets
1 cup (250 ml/8 fl oz) water
1 beef cube
1 teaspoon cornflour

Marinade
2 tablespoons soy sauce
1 tablespoon sherry
1 teaspoon sugar
2 tablespoon water
garlic, chopped
fresh ginger, chopped

Combine ingredients for marinade and add meat. Prepare vegetables, microwave for 2 minutes. Rub wok or electric frying pan with oil, add meat and quickly brown, add vegetables, add cup water. To the remaining marinade add 1 crushed beef cube and 1 teaspoon cornflour mixed with a little marinade to form a paste, add to boiling meat and vegetable mixture. Stir until thickened.
Serve with boiled rice.

SERVES 4

~

Meat Balls and Pasta

PREPARATION TIME: 10 MINUTES
FREEZING: SUITABLE

Meatballs
500 g (1 lb) minced topside
1 onion finely chopped
1 clove garlic
1 tablespoon plain flour
1 egg
½ cup chopped parsley

Sauce
1 × 440 g (14 oz) can salt-reduced tomato soup
1 teaspoon dried oregano

Mix meatball ingredients together and form into small meatballs about the size of a walnut. Quickly brown them in a heavy bottomed fry pan (you don't need any oil). Put meatballs aside.
Dilute the can of salt-reduced tomato soup with half a can of water, add meatballs and teaspoon of oregano. Bring to boil, heat gently for 10 minutes.
Serve over cooked macaroni or pasta of your choice.
Serve with tossed salad.

SERVES 4

~

Lamb Curry

PREPARATION TIME: 10 MINUTES
FREEZING: SUITABLE

500 g (1 lb) lamb fillet, diced
1 onion
2 teaspoons curry powder
2 large carrots
half a parsnip
2 large potatoes
1 cup frozen peas
1 tablespoon tomato sauce
1 tablespoon Worcestershire Sauce
1 tablespoon cornflour

Brown meat, onions and curry powder in saucepan. No oil is necessary. Dice carrots, parsnip and potatoes. Add all vegetables to meat. Add sauces. Cover with water and bring to the boil. Reduce heat and simmer with the lid on for 2 hours. Mix cornflour to a paste with a little water and add to boiling curry. Stir until thickened.
Serve with rice or potatoes.

SERVES 4

~

Gran's Savoury Mince

PREPARATION TIME: 20 MINUTES
FREEZING: SUITABLE

500 g (1 lb) minced topside steak
1 onion, finely diced
1 teaspoon curry powder (optional)
1 packet salt-reduced chicken noodle soup
1 cup (250 ml/8 fl oz) water
1 × 440 g (14 oz) can creamed sweet corn
1 large tomato sliced
½ cup dried bread crumbs
½ cup grated cheese

Preheat oven to 200°C (400°F).
Brown meat, onion, add curry powder and soup. Add 1 cup of water and cook until water has been absorbed. Remove from heat. Place half the meat mixture in a casserole dish, cover with half the corn. Repeat. Top with sliced tomato, bread crumbs and cheese.
Bake for 30 minutes.
Serve with carrot straws and Easy Potato Salad (page 77).

Serve with carrot straws and Easy Potato Salad (page 77).

SERVES 4

~

FAMILY PASTIE

PREPARATION TIME: 40 MINUTES
FREEZING: SUITABLE

Pastry
250 g (8 oz) smooth ricotta cheese
2 cups (250 g/8 oz) plain flour
1 egg
1 to 2 tablespoons cold water

Meat Filling
1 onion
2 large carrots
1 parsnip
500 g (1 lb) lean minced topside steak
½ cup frozen peas
black pepper (optional)

To make the pastry, add ricotta to sifted flour and stir evenly. Add lightly beaten egg and the water and stir until all the flour is mixed. Tip out on to a floured surface and gently knead. Cover in plastic wrap and refrigerate for one hour before use.
Preheat oven to 200°C (400°F).
Grate fresh vegetables. Brown the meat in a heavy bottomed frying pan. Add grated vegetables and mix through. Add peas and black pepper (if using).

Roll out pastry until 3–4 mm (⅛ in) thick. Place filling on pastry and pinch up the sides to make a large pastie shape. Place on a lightly greased oven tray and bake 25–30 minutes
or until golden brown.
Serve with mashed potato and peas.

SERVES 4

~

CHICKEN

APRICOT CHICKEN

PREPARATION TIME: 10 MINUTES
FREEZING: SUITABLE

2 chicken breasts with skin removed
half cup apricot jam
1 clove garlic
1 teaspoon finely chopped ginger
1 tablespoon soy sauce
2 tablespoons vinegar
1 × 440 g (14 oz) can apricot halves, drained

Cut chicken into cubes, mix remaining ingredients and add chicken. Marinate for at least half an hour. Thread onto 4 skewers, alternatively with piece of apricot. Place under a hot griller. Turn frequently and grill for 20 minutes. Also great on the barbecue.
Serve with Hot Potato Salad (page 78), French beans and grilled tomato halves.

Serve with Hot Potato Salad (page 78), French beans and grilled tomato halves.

SERVES 4

~

Chicken Lasagne

PREPARATION TIME: 40 MINUTES
FREEZING: SUITABLE

1 cooked chicken (either boil one or buy one
ready cooked)
1 small eggplant (aubergine)
2 zucchini
2 tomatoes
1 onion
½ green capsicum (pepper)
1 carrot
8–10 mushrooms
1 teaspoon oil
1 clove garlic
1 × 440 g (14 oz) can salt-reduced tomato soup
1 × 220 g (7 oz) (10 sheets) packet instant
lasagne noodles
1 quantity Cheese Sauce (page 79)

Preheat oven to 200°C (400°F).
Remove skin from chicken and discard.
Remove meat from chicken and dice. Set
aside. Peel and slice eggplant and
zucchini. Place in a colander on the sink.
Sprinkle with salt and leave. Slice the
remaining vegetables, thinly. Wash
eggplant and zucchini and shake well.
Heat oil in pan, add garlic then eggplant,
and brown each side of the eggplant well.
Repeat for all vegetables, excluding
mushrooms. Return vegetables to the pan,
add tomato soup plus half a can of water.
Add mushrooms. Simmer gently with lid
on for 5 minutes. Cool.
In a greased lasagne dish, spoon a little of
the vegetable sauce. Cover with lasagne
noodles. Cover with diced chicken then
vegetable sauce. Repeat until all the chicken
and sauce is used. Finish with noodles.
Pour cheese sauce over the top.
Bake for 1 hour.
Serve with a crisp salad and bread stick.

SERVES 6

Chicken and Cheese Bake

PREPARATION TIME: 10 MINUTES
FREEZING: SUITABLE

6 skinless chicken breast halves
3 slices of Swiss cheese cut in half
1 × 440 g (14 oz) can salt-reduced cream of
chicken soup
6 thin slices of tomato
1 teaspoon dried mixed herbs
½ cup bread crumbs

Preheat oven to 200° (400°F).
Lightly grease a shallow casserole dish.
Place chicken breasts in the dish, top with
cheese. Pour soup over and top with
tomato. Sprinkle herbs and bread crumbs
over tomatoes. Bake for 25–30 minutes.
Serve with boiled rice and vegetables.

SERVES 6

~

Chicken Quiche

PREPARATION TIME: 30 MINUTES
FREEZING: NOT SUITABLE

6 sheets filo pastry
250 g (½ lb) lean chicken mince
1 teaspoon oil
1 small onion, finely chopped
2 cloves garlic, crushed
1 teaspoon curry powder
4 eggs
2 cups (500 ml/16 fl oz) milk
1 tablespoon flour
250 g (8 oz) smooth ricotta cheese
3–4 spring onions (green onions), chopped

Preheat oven to 200° (400°F).
Line a lightly greased quiche plate approx
15 cm (6 in) with the 6 layers of filo
pastry. Trim the edges with scissors.
Brown chicken in oil with onion and
garlic, add curry powder.

Cook to evaporate any liquid. Allow mixture to get cold. Beat eggs with milk. Add flour, ricotta and spring onions to the cooled chicken mixture. Add beaten eggs and milk. Carefully pour the mixture into the quiche dish.
Bake for 40–50 minutes or until firm. Delicious hot or cold.
Serve with tossed salad.

SERVES 6

~

TINY CHICKEN SATAY PATTIES

PREPARATION TIME: 10 MINUTES
FREEZING: SUITABLE

500 g (1 lb) minced chicken
1 clove garlic
½ teaspoon curry powder
2 slices of fresh ginger finely chopped
½ teaspoon dried coriander
2 tablespoons smooth peanut butter
1 tablespoon salt-reduced soy sauce
1 tablespoon honey
1 egg
4 chopped spring onions (green onions)
1 tablespoon chopped parsley (optional)
2 tablespoons plain flour

Mix all ingredients. Lightly grease a pan and heat. Place teaspoons of mixture onto hot pan and flatten to make small patties. Turn over when brown to cook the other side.
Serve as a meal with a rice dish or in the school lunchbox.

MAKES APPROXIMATELY 36

PORK

Pork is an excellent lean meat and is no higher in fat than lean beef or chicken. There are many new cuts of pork which are easy to use.

PORK WITH APRICOT SAUCE

PREPARATION TIME: 20 MINUTES
FREEZING: NOT SUITABLE

4 lean pork fillets
1 tablespoon flour
½ teaspoon garlic powder
1 teaspoon oil

Sauce

1 × 440 g (14 oz) can apricot nectar
1–2 slices fresh ginger (optional)
1 tablespoon salt-reduced soy sauce
1 teaspoon cornflour

Flatten pork fillets and dip in flour mixed with garlic powder. Add oil to pan and quickly cook pork until done (about 5 minutes each side).
To make sauce combine all ingredients and stir over low heat until sauce thickens.
To serve, place a pork fillet on each plate and pour sauce over.
Serve with jacket potatoes and steamed vegetables.

SERVES 4

~

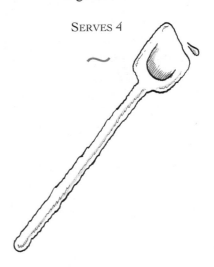

Sweet and Sour Pork

PREPARATION TIME: 30 MINUTES
FREEZING: NOT SUITABLE

500 g (1 lb) pork fillet
2 carrots
1 stick celery
1 onion
½ green capsicum (pepper)
1 × 440 g (14 oz) can crushed pineapple
(save juice for sauce)
2 tablespoons cornflour
2 teaspoons salt-reduced soy sauce

S a u c e
½ cup (125 g/4 oz) brown sugar
½ cup (125 ml/4 fl oz) white vinegar
½ cup (60 g/2 oz) cornflour
2 tablespoons salt-reduced soy sauce
juice of 1 × 440 g (14 oz) can crushed
pineapple
1 ½ cups water

Dice pork and place in saucepan, cover
with water and simmer until tender
(about 30 minutes). Drain water and set
meat aside to cool.
Cut vegetables into thin strips and
microwave on high for 2 minutes.
Combine all the sauce ingredients in a
large saucepan and stir over low heat until
thickened. Add drained crushed
pineapple. Remove from heat. Add cooked
vegetables. Add cornflour and soy sauce
to pork pieces. Brown in a lightly oiled hot
pan. Add pork pieces to sauce mixture.
Warm through, adjust flavouring to suit
your taste by adding either
a little more vinegar or sugar.
Serve with boiled rice.

SERVES 4

~

Fish

If you are lucky enough to catch your own
fresh fish, it is best enjoyed when it is cooked
simply. Clean the fish, dip in a little flour then
quickly cook in a little hot oil (about ½
teaspoon). Avoid putting batter on fish as
this soaks up copious amounts of oil and
makes a big mess in the kitchen — who
needs it! Fish is an excellent source of special
fatty acids which are thought to protect
against heart disease. Children usually enjoy
fish, preferring the less strongly flavoured
varieties. Fish with bones are not popular as
children find it a pain removing them. In
younger children, fish with small bones are
best avoided.
    As we are lazy cooks, these recipes use
canned fish either tuna or salmon but you
can use fresh fish if you prefer.

Tuna Slice

PREPARATION TIME: 20 MINUTES
FREEZING: NOT SUITABLE

1 × 425 g (13 oz) can tuna in spring water
4 eggs
2 cups (500 ml/16 fl oz) milk
1 cup (125 g/4 oz) self-raising flour
1 onion, finely chopped
1 × 440 g (14 oz) can drained sweet corn
kernels
2 cups grated cheese
½ cup chopped parsley

Preheat oven to 200°C (400°F).
Drain tuna, mash and place in casserole
dish. Beat eggs and milk. Add sifted flour
and remaining ingredients. Pour over
tuna. Bake for 40 minutes or until set.
Serve with rice and a tossed salad.

SERVES 4–6

~

FISH FINGERS

PREPARATION TIME: 40 MINUTES
FREEZING: SUITABLE

4 large potatoes
1 onion, finely chopped
1 × 425 g (13 oz) can tuna in spring water
1 carrot, grated
1 zucchini, grated
2 eggs
flour

Cook potatoes and onion until soft. Cool
then mash. Add remaining ingredients
except for flour. Shape into fingers or
patties or smaller balls. Roll in flour
and cook in a lightly oiled pan.
Serve with jacket potatoes and salad.

SERVES 4–6

~

BAKED FISH

PREPARATION TIME: 20 MINUTES
FREEZING: NOT SUITABLE

6 boneless fish fillets
juice of 1 lemon
1 onion, sliced
1 tomato, sliced
freshly ground black pepper (optional)

Preheat oven to 200°C (400°F).
Place fish on lightly greased foil. Sprinkle
with lemon juice, onion and tomato and
pepper (if using). Wrap and bake in the
oven for 40 minutes.
Serve with lemon slices, Easy Potato
Salad (page 77) and tossed salad.

SERVES 4–6

~

VEGETABLES AND SALAD

Try a variety of cooked and raw
vegetables. While only a limited number of
vegetables appear to be enjoyed by your
child, don't despair, with age comes an
increase in variety.

AVOCADO can be served as a spread on
sandwiches instead of butter or margarine.
Mix it with chicken or other meat and
mayonnaise for a great sandwich filling.
Mash with lemon juice and serve with
crackers as a snack.

AUBERGINE see EGGPLANT.

BEANS (GREEN) should be fresh and
crisp. Children sometimes enjoy them raw
or they can be lightly steamed or
microwaved. Use frozen or canned
varieties as well.

BEETROOT is something kids either love
or hate! It is usually enjoyed cooked and
pickled or canned. Tiny beetroots can be
steamed and served whole as a vegetable.
Jellied beetroot is delicious. Buy canned
shredded beetroot add 1 teaspoon of
gelatine dissolved in 1 tablespoon of hot
water to each cup of beetroot including
liquid.

BROAD BEANS can be podded and
lightly steamed or microwaved until
tender. Cook with sliced tomato and
chopped onion for a different flavour.

BROCCOLI should be cut into flowerets
and lightly steamed or microwaved.
Broccoli is great in stir-frys. Some children
enjoy this vegetable raw too. Delicious
with cheese sauce.

BRUSSELS SPROUTS are not the best loved vegetable but some children do become very fond of them. Don't overcook brussels sprouts as this develops their strong flavour. They should still be crisp. Microwave for 3 minutes then add chopped onion and diced tomato. Cook for a further 2 minutes.

CARROTS are very versatile vegetables. Here are six ideas:

- Cut carrots into thin strips and serve raw.
- Cut carrots into thin strips and add to dishes such as stir-frys and casseroles.
- Cut carrots into rings, microwave for 2 minutes add 1 teaspoon of honey while standing.
- Cook carrots with a small piece of parsnip, then mash together.
- Brush chunks of carrot with a little oil and bake in the oven for 1 hour.
- Mix strips of carrot with celery and snow peas, then add a little mayonnaise (delicious with grills).

CAULIFLOWER can be cut into flowerets and served raw. You can also lightly steam or microwave and serve mixed with carrot rings and broccoli. Serve with easy Cheese Sauce (see recipe page 79).

CABBAGE is best served to kids raw as in coleslaw or finely shredded and steamed or microwaved (for no more than a minute).

CELERY should be bought young and pale green and served simply by cutting into sticks. Great to munch on and very refreshing on a hot day. Add to casseroles and salads.

EGGPLANT can be cut into slices, placed in the colander, sprinkled lightly with salt and left to sit on the sink for about half an hour. This 'sweetens' the eggplant. Wash thoroughly and pat dry. Dip in flour and lightly fry in a little olive oil. Serve with a sprinkle of Parmesan cheese.

LEEKS should be washed thoroughly. Pull the layers apart and wash under running cold water. Cut up finely and add to soups. Steam or microwave and serve with White Sauce (see recipe page 78). Can be used in place of onion for a slightly different flavour.

LETTUCE is something children enjoy munching on. Add to sandwiches, or use as part of a main meal with other raw vegetables.

MARROW look interesting on the plate. Choose baby marrows and lightly steam or microwave.

ONION is not generally well-liked by children but adds flavour to dishes.

PEAS are loved by most children. Serve fresh, frozen or canned. Delicious hot or cold. Add to potato salad, casseroles.

POTATO is a great food, full of good nutrients. Serve as a snack or with meals.

PUMPKIN should be steamed or microwaved until tender. It is delicious baked in the oven. Pumpkin varieties are numerous and they are easy to grow. If you have room in your back garden throw some pumpkin seeds on the ground and let nature do the rest. Some pumpkin varieties take over the back yard but there are some which don't need much room. Ask your plant nursery for advice.

SPINACH and SILVER BEET should be chopped and steamed or microwaved until tender. Use in stir-fries and casseroles.

SWEET CORN is a very popular vegetable with children. Serve as 'corn on the cob' or use canned varieties.

SQUASH and SWEDE are used as for pumpkin.

TOMATO is a popular vegetable. Serve cooked or raw. Grow your own tiny tomatoes in a pot. The children will love eating them straight from the bush.

ZUCCHINI can be served cooked with tomato or used in recipes. See vegetarian recipes (page 80).

STUFFED POTATOES

PREPARATION TIME: 10 MINUTES
FREEZING: NOT SUITABLE

4 medium sized potatoes
2 lean rashers bacon
½ cup grated cheese
2 teaspoons reduced-salt French onion soup (packet)
1 tablespoon Easy Mayonnaise (page 78)

Scrub potatoes and cut a cross on the top. Microwave for 8 minutes or steam for 40 minutes. Allow to 'sit' for a further 8 minutes. Dice bacon finely and microwave for 10 seconds or quickly dry fry. Carefully scoop out potato and mash in a bowl. Add all other ingredients. Pile back into potato shells and microwave for 1 minute or bake in oven at 220°C (425°F) for 10 minutes.

SERVES 4

~

'ANNE'S' POTATOES

PREPARATION TIME: 10 MINUTES
FREEZING: NOT SUITABLE

4 large potatoes
1 onion, sliced
½ cup milk

Peel potatoes and cut into thin slices. Layer potato and onion into a casserole dish. Pour milk over. Bake in the oven for 45 minutes or microwave for 10 minutes using a microwave dish.

SERVES 4–6

~

EASY POTATO SALAD

PREPARATION TIME: 10 MINUTES
FREEZING: NOT SUITABLE

4 large potatoes
1 large onion
2 eggs, hard boiled
1 cup Easy Mayonnaise (page 78)

Cook potatoes and onion by boiling or microwaving. Vegetables must be soft. Mash together roughly with the cooked eggs. Stir in mayonnaise. Chill. Serve with grills.

Hot Potato Salad

PREPARATION TIME: 20 MINUTES
FREEZING: NOT SUITABLE

4 large potatoes, diced
1 large onion finely chopped
2 spring onions (green onions) chopped
2 lean rashers of bacon
1 cup Easy Mayonnaise (page 78)

Preheat oven to 200°C (400°F).
Cook potato and onion. Place in flat dish
such as a lasagne dish. Add all other
ingredients. Bake in the oven for
10 minutes.

SERVES 4–6

~

Baked Pumpkin

PREPARATION TIME: 10 MINUTES
FREEZING: NOT SUITABLE

Preheat oven to 220°C (425°F).
Cut pumpkin pieces into small chunks.
Brush with oil and bake in a hot oven for
45 minutes.

ALLOW 3–4 SMALL CHUNKS PER PERSON

~

Delicious Diced Pumpkin

Dice pumpkin, steam or microwave
3–4 minutes until tender. Sprinkle with
chopped parsley and ½ teaspoon nutmeg.
Some children may prefer this mashed.
Parsnip should be cut into pieces, brushed
with a little oil and baked in the oven for
35–40 minutes at 220°C (425°F).
Cook with carrot and mash together for a
different flavour.

Easy sauces

A sauce can add extra flavour as well as
moisture to a food. Children often prefer
moist food. Try some of these easy recipes.
Many of them are incorporated in other
recipes along the way.

Easy Mayonnaise

PREPARATION TIME: 3 MINUTES
FREEZING: NOT SUITABLE

1 × 415 g (13 oz) can skimmed condensed milk
¼ teaspoon dry mustard
1 cup white vinegar

Empty condensed milk into a large jar
with a screw top lid. Add mustard and add
in vinegar. If you prefer a thinner
consistency, add more vinegar. Store in
the refrigerator. This mixture will thicken
up on standing, add more vinegar if
necessary.
This recipe is delicious and fat free. Use
for salads, on sandwiches or add crushed
garlic and use as a dip with fresh carrot
and celery sticks.

MAKES 1 JAR

~

White Sauce

PREPARATION TIME: 15 MINUTES
FREEZING: SUITABLE

2 cups (500 ml/16 fl oz) reduced-fat milk
2 tablespoons cornflour

Bring milk to the boil, mix cornflour to a
thin paste with a little cold water and add
to milk. Stir until it thickens.

MAKES 2 CUPS (500 ML/16 FL OZ)

CHEESE SAUCE

PREPARATION TIME: 15 MINUTES
FREEZING: SUITABLE

2 cups (500 ml/16 fl oz) reduced-fat milk
2 tablespoons cornflour
½ cup grated cheese

Bring milk to the boil, mix cornflour to a thin paste with a little cold water and add to milk. Stir until it thickens. Add grated cheese.

MAKES 2 CUPS (500 ML/16 FL OZ)

CUSTARD

PREPARATION TIME: 15 MINUTES
FREEZING: SUITABLE

2 cups (500 ml/16 fl oz) reduced-fat milk
2 tablespoons custard powder
1 tablespoon sugar

Bring milk to the boil. Mix custard powder to a thin paste with a little cold water, add sugar, and then add to milk. Stir until it thickens.

MAKES 2 CUPS (500 ML/16 FL OZ)

~

FRUIT SAUCE

PREPARATION TIME: 5 MINUTES
FREEZING: SUITABLE

juice of 2 oranges
2 tablespoons salt-reduced soy sauce
2 teaspoons honey
½ teaspoon garlic powder
¼ cup water
1 teaspoon cornflour

Combine the first five ingredients in a saucepan and stir over a gentle heat. Mix cornflour with a little cold water, add to the sauce and stir until it thickens. Serve with grills and roast meats, or as a dip for pieces of meat and vegetable.

MAKES 1 CUP (250 ML/8 FL OZ)

Vegetarian Meals

You may wish to follow a vegetarian diet that is suitable for the whole family. A diet that includes dairy foods and eggs as well as breads and cereals, fruit and vegetables is suitable for a growing child. See 'Ages and Stages' (page 15) for quantities of 'meat substitutes'. Vegetarian diets are very bulky because they are made up of more breads and cereals, fruits and vegetables. It is necessary to serve your child milk and meat substitutes first in a meal so that essential calcium and iron are consumed before the child becomes too full.

A diet excluding dairy foods as well as meat should be analysed for its nutritional adequacy by a dietitian. When the range of foods is reduced too much in a child's diet, there can be serious problems with growth and development, including mental growth and maturity.

You don't have to be 'vegetarian' to enjoy delicious and nutritious vegetarian meals. Try some of these recipes.

Zucchini and Parmesan Cheese

PREPARATION TIME: 30 MINUTES
FREEZER: NOT SUITABLE

6–8 young, tender zucchini
4 eggs, beaten
flour, about ½ cup
grated Parmesan cheese

Peel zucchini and cut lengthwise into thin slices, place in a colander, lightly sprinkle with salt and leave for half an hour on the sink. This 'sweetens' the zucchini. Wash thoroughly under running cold water. Shake well. Heat a lightly greased pan. Flour each piece, dip in beaten egg and place in pan.

Turn over to brown both sides. Place on serving dish and lightly sprinkle with grated Parmesan cheese. Place in low oven to keep warm.
Serve with Hot Potato Salad (page 78) and tossed green salad.

SERVES 6

~

Vegetable Casserole

PREPARATION TIME: 10 MINUTES
FREEZING: SUITABLE

2 large carrots, cut into rings
half parsnip, chopped
2 sticks celery, diced
1 large onion, cut into rings
1 × 440 g (14 oz) can creamed corn
4 large potatoes, sliced
½ cup (125 ml/4 fl oz) reduced-fat milk

Preheat oven to 200°C (400°F). Combine all the ingredients. Place in a lightly greased casserole dish and cook with the lid on in a moderate oven for 45–50 minutes. Serve as an accompaniment to meat or fish or as a meal with crusty bread.

SERVES 4 AS A MEAL

~

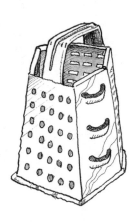

BEANS 'N' THINGS

Dried beans and lentils are a delicious source of protein and fibre, and most kids love them. There is a variety of canned cooked beans such as baked beans, kidney beans, chick peas, mixed-bean mix. There is also the dried variety, which require soaking overnight and then boiling before adding to dishes.

BEANS WITH RICE

PREPARATION TIME: 15 MINUTES
FREEZING: NOT SUITABLE

½ cup (90 g/3 oz) rice
1 teaspoon oil
1 clove garlic, crushed
1 onion, finely diced
1 cup frozen French beans
2 carrots, cut into thin strips
1 × 440 g (14 oz) can beans of your choice, drained
chopped parsley

Boil water and cook rice. Heat oil in pan. Add crushed garlic and onion, stir quickly. Add other vegetables, reduce heat and cook with the lid on until vegetables are just tender. Add rice and stir through. Lastly add drained beans and chopped parsley. Quickly heat through, add a little water to prevent sticking.

SERVES 4–6

~

PASTA WITH CHICKPEA SAUCE

PREPARATION TIME: 5 MINUTES
FREEZING: SUITABLE

2 cups (90 g/3 oz) pasta of your choice
1 × 440 g (14 oz) can tomatoes
1 large onion, finely diced
1 clove garlic, crushed
1 teaspoon oregano
2 tablespoons tomato paste
2 zucchini, finely chopped
2 carrots, finely chopped
chopped mushrooms (optional)
1 × 440 g (14 oz) can chickpeas

Cook pasta. Roughly mash tomatoes and combine all ingredients except for mushrooms and chickpeas. Simmer gently for half an hour, add mushrooms and drained chickpeas. Heat through. Serve over pasta. Sprinkle with Parmesan cheese.

SERVES 4–6

~

STUFFED MUSHROOMS

PREPARATION TIME: 5 MINUTES
FREEZING: NOT SUITABLE

½ cup dried breadcrumbs
½ teaspoon dried mixed herbs
1 small onion, finely diced
12 large mushroom caps

Preheat oven to 220°C (425°F). Combine breadcrumbs, herbs and onion. Place mixture in each mushroom. Place on a lightly greased tray. Bake in oven for 10 minutes.

SERVES 6 (TWO MUSHROOMS PER PERSON)

MACARONI CHEESE

PREPARATION TIME: 10 MINUTES
FREEZING: SUITABLE

2 cups macaroni
1 quantity of Cheese Sauce (page 79)
2 teaspoons onion flakes

Cook macaroni in boiling water. Drain into a colander and run cold water through to separate noodles. Place in a casserole dish. Make up cheese sauce add onion flakes pour over macaroni. Mix through. Heat in the oven for 20 minutes. Serve with a crisp salad.
Add extras to suit your family:
• ½ cup of corn kernels
• ½ cup cooked peas
• ½ cup diced cooked carrots
• Add all 3!

SERVES 4

For something sweet

'FILLERS' — SOMETHING EXTRA FOR THE LUNCHBOX

Children enjoy something sweet either between meals or to finish off a meal. Commercial cakes and biscuits are very high in fat and sugar and so are most home-made recipes. Here are a few recipes where the fat and sugar have been reduced to make a tasty 'filler'.

MUFFINS

PREPARATION TIME: 10 MINUTES
FREEZING: SUITABLE

½ cup sultanas
½ cup dried apricots, diced
(mixed dried fruit can be used instead of sultanas and dried apricots)
1½ cups (375 ml/12 fl oz) milk
¼ cup (60 g/2 oz) sugar
1 egg
1 cup (125 g/4 oz) self-raising flour
1 teaspoon cinnamon

Preheat oven to 200°C (400°F). Heat fruit in milk. Bring to the boil. Allow to cool. Add sugar, egg and flour sifted with cinnamon. Stir until flour is just combined. Place spoonfuls into greased muffin tins. Bake for 25 minutes. Leave in tin for 10 minutes to cool.

MAKES 12 MUFFINS

~

EASY BUTTERSCOTCH CAKE

PREPARATION TIME: 10 MINUTES
FREEZING: SUITABLE

60 g (2 oz) margarine
½ cup (85 g/3 oz) brown sugar
2 eggs
½ cup stewed apple
1 cup (250 ml/8 fl oz) milk
2 cups (250 g/8 oz) self-raising flour
1 teaspoon cinnamon
half teaspoon ginger
half teaspoon mixed spice
1 tablespoon golden syrup

Preheat oven to 200°C (400°F). Cream margarine and sugar. Add golden syrup and eggs, and beat well. Add apple and milk. Stir in flour sifted with spices. Pour into a greased and lined loaf tin. Bake for 45 minutes.

ORANGE COCONUT COOKIES

PREPARATION TIME: 20 MINUTES
FREEZING: NOT SUITABLE

60 g (2 oz) margarine
1 cup (220 g/7 oz) caster sugar
2 teaspoons grated orange rind
1 egg
½ cup (125 g/4 oz) ricotta cheese
1½ cups (185 g/6 oz) plain flour
½ teaspoon bicarbonate of soda
2 tablespoons desiccated coconut (for rolling
cookies in)

Preheat oven to 200°C (400°F).
Cream margarine and sugar. Add orange
rind and egg. Beat well. Stir in ricotta and
sifted flour and soda. Mix well. Roll
walnut sized pieces in coconut, place on a
lightly greased tray. Bake for
15–20 minutes until coconut is golden
brown. Slightly cool on tray
before removing.
Ricotta cheese is a handy ingredient to
substitute in recipes where
sour cream is used.

MAKES 30 COOKIES

MEAL FINISHERS

Puddings were once part of everyone's
meal but now they are a special treat.
These meal finishers are nutritious
without unnecessary fat.

BAKED ORANGE BREAD PUDDING

PREPARATION TIME: 10 MINUTES
FREEZING: NOT SUITABLE

2 thick slices bread
1 × 375 ml (12 fl oz) can evaporated milk
¼ cup (55 g/2 oz) caster sugar
2 eggs
2 teaspoons grated orange rind

Preheat oven to 200°C (400°F).
Remove crusts from bread and cut into
cubes. Place in a lightly greased casserole
dish. Combine the remaining ingredients
and whisk together. Pour over bread.
Bake for 45 minutes.

SERVES 6

~

EASY RICE PUDDING

PREPARATION TIME: 5 MINUTES
FREEZING: NOT SUITABLE

½ cup (110 g/3½ oz) rice
1 × 375 ml (12 fl oz) can evaporated milk or
use fresh milk
¼ cup (60 g/2 oz) sugar
½ cup sultanas

Preheat oven to 200°C (400°F).
Cook rice and drain well. Combine all
ingredients. Place in casserole dish. Cook
for 10 minutes in the oven or in the
microwave for 5 minutes on high.

SERVES 6

BAKED APPLES

PREPARATION TIME: 10 MINUTES
FREEZING: NOT SUITABLE

6 Granny Smith apples
6 prunes or dried apricots
½ cup sultanas
½ teaspoon cinnamon
water

Core apples. Place a prune or apricot at
the bottom of each apple to act as a 'plug'.
Mix sultanas with cinnamon and fill each
cavity. Place in a dish with 1 cup of water.
Microwave on high for 8 minutes or bake
in the oven at 200°C (400°F) for
30 minutes.

SERVES 6

~

FRUIT CRUMBLE

PREPARATION TIME: 5 MINUTES
FREEZING: NOT SUITABLE

1 × 440 g (14 oz) can pie apples, apricots or
peaches
½ cup wheat flakes
½ cup (45 g/1 ½ oz) coconut
½ teaspoon cinnamon

Preheat oven to 200°C (400°F).
Place fruit into a pie dish. Lightly crush
the cereal, mix with coconut and
cinnamon, sprinkle over the top of fruit.
Bake for 10 minutes.
Serve with custard or reduced-fat
yoghurt.

SERVES 6

STEAMED JAM PUDDING

PREPARATION TIME: 10 MINUTES
FREEZING: NOT SUITABLE

4 tablespoons jam
1 packet plain cake mix

Place jam in the bottom of a lightly
greased pudding bowl. Make up cake mix
according to directions. Pour over jam.
Cover with foil and place in a saucepan
half full of water. Place saucepan lid on
top. Bring water to the boil, reduce the
heat and simmer for 45–50 minutes.
Remove from heat. Place on a dinner plate
and invert pudding.
Jam will now be on the top.
Serve with custard, yoghurt or ice-cream.

SERVES 6

~

COLD DESSERTS

BERRY SALAD

PREPARATION TIME: 5 MINUTES
FREEZING: NOT SUITABLE

1 cup of frozen blueberries
1 cup of frozen raspberries
1 cup of frozen strawberries
1 × 1 kg (2 lb) tub vanilla yoghurt

Allow berries to almost thaw, about half
an hour. Stir through yoghurt. Spoon into
glass dessert bowls and serve immediately.

SERVES 6

~

BAKED BANANAS

PREPARATION TIME: 5 MINUTES
FREEZING: NOT SUITABLE

6 bananas
2 tablespoons brown sugar
juice of 1 lemon

Preheat oven to 200°C (400°F).
Split bananas lengthwise and place in a
lightly greased pie dish. Sprinkle with
brown sugar and lemon juice. Bake for 10
minutes.
Serve warm with custard or reduced-fat
yoghurt.

SERVES 6

~

PINEAPPLE DESSERT

PREPARATION TIME: 15 MINUTES
FREEZING: NOT SUITABLE

1 × 375 g (12 oz) can crushed pineapple
1 quantity Custard (page 79)
1 packet pineapple jelly
pineapple rings, to decorate

Drain pineapple and set aside juice. Place
pineapple at the bottom of a large dessert
bowl. Make up jelly using juice and water
to make up to 2 cups. Stir through and
pour carefully over pineapple. Allow to
set. Make 1 quantity of custard. When
cold, pour over pineapple jelly mixture.
Refrigerate. Decorate with canned
pineapple rings.
Serve with ice-cream.

SERVES 6–8

Healthy drinks

WHAT TO DRINK?

Ideally water is the best thirst quencher but nourishing drinks can be a good way to use up the food allowances (see Chapter Two) and are a healthy treat.

Milk shakes are always popular and provide essential calcium.

MANGO SHAKE

PREPARATION TIME: 5 MINUTES

1 cup (250 ml/8 fl oz) milk
1 scoop ice-cream
1 × 220 g (7 oz) can drained mango slices (or use fresh mango)

Place all ingredients in a blender and blend until smooth.
Serve in tall glasses with a straw.

SERVES 4

VARIATIONS

Substitute 1 can drained crushed pineapple or 1 punnet fresh strawberries washed and hulled for mango.

~

Party time

BIRTHDAY PARTIES — DARE TO BE DIFFERENT!

Overheard this conversation recently:
Mother: 'Well, Jenny, did you have a good time at Jodie's party? What did you have to eat?'

Jenny (shrugs): 'It was OK. Just the usual junk.'

Children in primary school seem to go to a lot of birthday parties, but there is nothing as exciting as when the party is for you! Unfortunately, most party foods fall into the junk food category, and interestingly enough, kids prefer different foods from the same old thing. After all there is a limit to how many sausage rolls and hot dogs kids can eat or, even more boring these days, is that many birthday parties are held at fast food outlets. It's OK sometimes but when everyone is doing it!

The following foods have all been tried at birthday parties with enormous success and the minimum of fuss and expense.

NIBBLES

Kids like to nibble on foods, so make platters of bite sized foods. Apart from the recipes that follow, see also Meat Balls (page 70).

CELERY AND CARROT STICKS WITH CHEESE

3 large crisp celery sticks
1 large carrot
cubes of cheese (you can buy these already prepared)

Wash celery thoroughly and cut into sticks, peel and wash carrot and cut the same size as the celery.
Arrange on a platter with cheese cubes. Serve with dips such as hommus or tzatziki, and watch the kids tuck in.

~

CHICKEN PLATTER

Serve a platter of cold cooked chicken pieces with tomato wedges, sliced hard boiled eggs and dried fruit such as prunes, apricots and apple. Garnish with lots of fresh parsley.

~

SURPRISE PARCELS

PREPARATION TIME: 10 MINUTES
FREEZING: NOT SUITABLE

4 cups cooked chicken, chopped
2 spring onions (green onions), finely chopped
2 cups finely chopped celery
1 cup chopped walnuts
½ cup Easy Mayonnaise (page 78)
1 packet Lavache bread (8 pieces)

Mix chicken, spring onion (green onion), celery, walnuts and mayonnaise. Divide into eight parts. Spread each part on one piece of Lavache bread. Fold the bottom edge ¼ way up then fold in on one side then the top and roll to make a parcel.
Allow one parcel per person.
Filling alternatives: Substitute a drained 440 g (14 oz) can tuna in spring water for chicken; or delete walnuts, add drained crushed pineapple and substitute 250 g (8 oz) diced lean ham for chicken.

SERVES 8

~

THEME PARTIES

Kids love to dress up so a party with a theme is always a winner. Keep the themes simple as not all parents will share your enthusiasm for a complicated costume! To get you started, a couple of examples follow.
JURASSIC PARK Cook jaffles with fillings of baked beans and call them 'dinosaur eggs'. Cut sandwiches into the shapes of footprints.
COLOUR PARTIES A Green Party, where everyone dresses in green and all the food is green! Very easy! Serve lots of vegetable platters. Puree kiwi fruit, mix with soda water for drinks. Serve green apples stuffed and baked for dessert. You are only limited by your own imagination.
Warning: Don't resort to food colouring, as this may affect some children. There are plenty of coloured foods provided by nature.

Sweet treats

A birthday cake is a must. It is difficult to make a decent cake without a lot of fat so go ahead and make your child's favourite one. After all the other healthy foods, only a small portion will be eaten by each child.

Most cakes at birthday parties are ignored, although there will always be a few children who like sweet things.

Try a fruit platter instead. Include fruit in season as well as dried fruit and nuts (for older children). Serve with a pot of fruit yoghurt so that children can dip each piece of fruit into the yoghurt.

A simple ice-cream in a cone is always acceptable for kids of all ages — and there is no washing up!

Drinks for a crowd

Fruit Punch

Preparation time: 5 minutes

2 cups (500 ml/15 fl oz) cold black tea

4 cups (1 litre/32 fl oz) pineapple juice

2 cups (500 ml/15 fl oz) orange juice

2 × 1.25 litre (2 pints) bottles low-joule dry ginger ale

2 × 1.25 litre (2 pints) bottles low-joule lemonade

ice cubes

slices of fresh oranges and lemons (2 of each)

Mix together first three ingredients. Fill a jug half full with this mixture add equal parts of dry ginger and lemonade. Add ice and slices of orange and lemon. This is economical for a thirsty crowd.

Makes 8 litres (14 pints)

Answers to questions parents commonly ask

White-bread worries

Q: My child refuses to eat wholemeal bread. If I make his school lunch with anything else but white bread he brings it home untouched.

A: It is better to eat white bread than no bread at all! Children need at least 6–8 slices of bread each day. While wholemeal bread certainly is a lot higher in fibre than white bread, there is still *some* fibre in white bread. Foods such as wholegrain breakfast cereal, fruits and vegetables will help to increase your child's fibre intake.

Vegetable trauma

Q: My child just hates vegetables and refuses to eat anything that looks remotely green. What should I do? I am sick of fighting with him all the time.

A: The best way to get over this problem is to include vegetables in interesting ways. Stir-frys are popular with primary school children and include a lot of vegetables.

For some strange reason parents tend to view the eating of vegetables as only eating cooked vegetables. Many children prefer raw vegetables or salads instead. If your child is not wild about vegies, place a platter of chopped, raw vegetables on the table and let him choose — suggest that he choose three different colours.

Soup is another way to incorporate vegetables into your child's diet. Casseroles and pasta dishes all 'carry' finely chopped or grated vegetables. Always serve vegetables as part of your child's meal. If they are not eaten, remove them from the table but continue to offer them at each meal. Sooner or later your child will eat something or other. If you eat lots of vegies yourself, your child will end up enjoying them too.

Healthy ideas for school fund-raisers

Parents these days need to spend a lot of time and effort to raise funds for extra programs, sporting equipment, library books and so on. There is probably not a week goes by without a request to buy lamingtons, chocolates, or some other item. It would be remiss of us not to offer a healthy alternative to all the 'junk food drives' that hit us each week.

Suggest some of these fund-raising ideas to your Parents & Friends Association:

- Apple drives

- Orange drives

- Plant drives (contact your local plant nursery and arrange to buy a range of easy to grow plants at a negotiated cost, and sell them at a slightly higher price)

- Hot cross bun drives

- Send the money to save baking a cake drives

- Personalised stationery drives

- Healthy food day (each family donates a healthy food item, the class makes the lunch then buys it)

- Eat no junk for a week or a month and get sponsors

- Healthy eatathon (fine those students who eat high-fat, high-salt foods; have only fresh fruit and vegetables for morning recess once a week at the canteen)

- Exercise days

- Walkathons

- Skipping competition

CHAPTER TEN

A TO Z EASY REFERENCE

ACIDOPHILUS

Acidophilus or lactobacillus acidophilus
(A culture) is a natural bacteria in our
guts. It is also one of the cultures used in
combination with bifidobacterium
(B culture), also a natural bacteria in our
guts, to produce a new range of 'health'
yoghurts. Yoghurts or other fermented
products containing A and B cultures are
said to have many health benefits
including: maintaining the right balance of
gut bacteria, protecting the gut against
infection from other bacteria, relieving
constipation, restoring the natural gut
bacteria after diarrhoea caused by
antibiotics, protection against the vaginal
yeast infection thrush, and protection
against colon cancer.

ADDITIVES, FOOD

Food additives are not eaten as foods, but
are intentionally added to foods to improve
their keeping qualities, taste, texture, and
appearance; to improve nutritional value;
and to assist with processing. Additives
have been used in our foods for centuries,
the earliest ones being salt, sugar, smoke,
vinegar and spices.

The types, purity and quantities of
additives allowed in foods is strictly set
out in government Food Standards Codes.
Any processed food that contains additives
will have them listed in the ingredient list.
The class name is given followed by the
name of the additive or its additive
number. A list of approved additives is
available from government departments.
For people with food sensitivities, the
additive numbering system makes
selecting foods easier.

ALLERGY

Food allergy is an unpleasant reaction to a
food protein that involves the immune
system. Harmful antibodies are produced
by the body as a defence against a foreign
protein and cause symptoms such as
swelling, itching, wheezing, vomiting,
tummy pains and diarrhoea. Symptoms
usually occur within 1–2 hours. Some of
the common foods causing food allergy
include cow's milk, eggs, peanuts, fish,
wheat and soy. While food allergy is often
regarded as the cause of children's food
problems, the incidence is low
(about 2–5%).

Food allergy does tend to run in families
and is most common in infants and
children where there is a history of known
allergy and allergy symptoms such as
eczema, asthma and hay fever. Most
children grow out of their allergies. If an
allergy is suspected consult with your
doctor or dietitian.

AMINO ACIDS

These are the 'building blocks' of proteins. Amino acids are linked together by peptide bonds to form the long chains of protein. Of the 23 amino acids, 8 are essential. This is because they must come from food as our bodies cannot make them. The essential amino acids are methionine, threonine, tryptophan, isoleucine, leucine, phenylalanine, lysine and valine.

Animal proteins (meat, fish, milk, eggs) are often referred to as 'first-class proteins' because they contain all the essential amino acids. Vegetable proteins, on the other hand, are referred to as 'second-class proteins' because they are missing one or more of the essential amino acids. However by combining various vegetable proteins (cereal, vegetable, legumes) together or with animal proteins, a protein value equivalent to first-class proteins can be obtained. This is the principle used in vegetarian diets, for example: baked beans on toast (legumes and grains), rice with sesame seeds (grains and seeds), peanut butter on bread (nuts and grains), cheese on bread (animal protein and grains).

ANAEMIA

Iron deficiency anaemia is the most common nutritional deficiency in the world. Anaemia is the last stage of a process of falling iron stores in the body, with no iron in the bone marrow, very small red blood cells and haemoglobin levels below the reference range. Symptoms include tiredness, pallor, reduced physical performance, reduced immunity and shortness of breath. Groups at risk of iron deficiency anaemia include young children, teenage girls and women. Australian studies show that a high proportion of 10–15 year olds consume less than the Recommended Dietary

Intake of iron, and that the risk of deficiency rises about five times between ages 12 and 15 years. Risk is minimised by including iron-rich foods in the diet, particularly red meats (beef, lamb), which are the best source of available iron, chicken, pork, fish, iron-fortified breakfast cereals, and breads, legumes, fruits and vegetables.

ANOREXIA NERVOSA

This is an eating disorder where voluntary starvation is used to lose weight. This severe and distressing illness is characterised by a very low body weight and a refusal to gain weight to within a normal healthy weight range. Some of the weight-losing behaviours include refusal to eat, over exercising, vomiting and use of laxatives and diuretics. Anorexia can have detrimental effects on the body, including malnutrition, loss of menstruation and fertility, delayed and stunted growth, osteoporosis, hair loss, heart and kidney disorders, and can lead to death. Psychological disturbances are also present, such as depression and withdrawal from friends and family. If anorexia is suspected, see your local doctor, specialist or dietitian.

ANTI-OXIDANTS

Anti-oxidants stop oxidation, a chemical reaction requiring oxygen which takes place in body cells. Some of the products of oxidation, such as free radicals, are damaging to cells and are being linked with diseases associated with aging, cancer and heart disease. Anti-oxidants are thus being studied because of their potential to prevent these diseases. The best known anti-oxidants are vitamins C,

E and beta carotene. They are found in fruits, vegetables and grains. It appears that anti-oxidants obtained from foods have a better protective effect than those obtained from vitamin tablets, though this is still being investigated. It may be that other components in foods, not just the anti-oxidant vitamins, are having a protective effect. However, based on available evidence, it is suggested that we eat at least five serves a day of fruits and vegetables.

ARTIFICIAL SWEETENERS

Artificial sweeteners are used in place of sugar (usually sucrose, table sugar) to sweeten foods so that sugar intake and/or dietary calories/kilojoules are reduced. They are 30 to 2000 times sweeter than sugar and, unlike sugar, do not cause dental caries. Common artificial sweeteners include saccharin, cyclamates, Nutrasweet (aspartame) and Splenda (sucralose). All sweeteners must be thoroughly tested for safety before being approved by governments for consumer use and inclusion in processed foods.

Artificial sweeteners are useful in diabetic and weight-reduction diets. However they are not necessary for healthy, growing, active children. A safe daily level of intake has been calculated for each artificial sweetener to ensure complete safety if consumed throughout life. The daily amount set for children is much lower than for adults. (See also Nutrasweet, Splenda.)

ASCORBIC ACID (VITAMIN C)

Ascorbic acid is also called vitamin C and is essential for maintaining the health of connective tissues and blood vessels. A lack of vitamin C causes bleeding gums, bruising, weak muscles and infections. Vitamin C is also a natural anti-oxidant that counteracts potentially damaging compounds formed in the body. Population studies have shown that high levels of vitamin C may be protective against heart disease. Vitamin C also enhances the absorption of iron from non-meat foods such as vegetables, legumes, grains (breads, breakfast cereals, rice, pasta etc.) and fruits by up to 50%.

Vitamin C is necessary during growth. It is not stored in the body but must be supplied every day. It is easily destroyed by heat and cooking. Sources of vitamin C include citrus fruits (oranges, mandarins, lemons, grapefruit), capsicum, broccoli, paw paw, strawberries, mango, tomatoes, potatoes, cabbage, cauliflower. Vitamin C requirements for 5–12 year olds are easily met by eating half a medium orange or ¼ cup fruit juice.

ASPARTAME

Aspartame is made from the amino acids (protein 'building blocks') aspartic acid and phenylalanine. While individually these amino acids are not sweet, combined they have a sweetening power 180 times that of sugar. Aspartame has been rigorously tested over the years and has been found to be safe for children, adults and pregnant and lactating women. It is not recommended for those with the genetic disorder phenylketonuria.

Aspartame is approved for use in low-joule (energy) foods such as soft drinks, yoghurts, cordials, desserts and confectionery. Its brand name is Nutrasweet.

ASTHMA AND DIET

Controversy surrounds the association of asthma and diet. However while food allergy (a protein sensitivity) is rare, sensitivity to chemicals naturally present in foods is more common, affecting about 10–20% of asthmatics. The most common provokers include aspirin (found in medicines and cough mixtures), sulphites (found in 'preservative added' commercial fruit juices and drinks, dried fruit, potato chips, sausages, cheese, wine, vinegar), MSG and food dyes. Dietary management may be needed to assist with the control of asthma. Always consult with your doctor or dietitian.

BACTERIA

Bacteria are micro organisms that occur everywhere, including in and on the body. Some are harmful and can cause tummy upsets and diarrhoea when they multiply to large numbers in food that has been left exposed at room temperature. It is important to handle and store food at the correct temperature to keep food safe. Other bacteria are not harmful and are used to make yoghurt (see Acidophilus) from milk or add flavour to foods like sauerkraut and pickles. Bacteria is naturally present in our gut. It produces vitamin K for the clotting of blood and in the large intestine breaks down dietary fibre.

BAKED BEANS

Baked beans are made from navy beans that are cooked with various flavoured sauces (usually tomato). They are a nutritious and economical food, being high in dietary fibre (4.8%), high in protein (4.6%), low in fat (0.5%) and having no cholesterol. They make an excellent replacement for meat in vegetarian diets and for children who don't like eating meat.

BANANAS

Bananas are a popular fruit for children and are also nutritious, supplying complex carbohydrate and dietary fibre, sugars and vitamins B1, B2, C and niacin. They are a rich source of potassium and, like all fruit, are low in fat and salt. Unripe bananas (green) contain predominantly starch, which is converted to sugars during ripening. Ripe bananas are best to eat and more digestible. Bananas do contain amines, which may cause reactions in some sensitive children.

BARLEY

Barley is one of the oldest cereal grains and today most of it is used for stock food. It is also an important source of malt in the brewing of beer and as a flavouring in foods. Pearl barley, used as a thickener for soups, casseroles and desserts, has been the traditional way of eating barley. Barley is a nutritious grain, containing complex carbohydrate (starch) and dietary fibre along with B group vitamins, vitamin E and important minerals such as potassium, calcium, iron and zinc. It is low in fat and high in insoluble dietary fibre and has been shown to lower cholesterol levels. The bioflavinoids, vitamin E, selenium and phytate in barley act as anti-oxidants and may protect against cancer. As barley contains small amounts of gluten, it is not suitable for those on gluten-free diets, such as coeliacs.

BENZOATES OR BENZOIC ACID

The benzoates are a group of additives that function as preservatives, thereby prolonging a food's shelf life. The common ones are benzoic acid (additive number 210), sodium benzoate (211), potassium benzoate (212) and calcium benzoate (213). They may be added to fruit juices, fruit juice drinks, low-joule jams, soft drinks, flavoured syrups and toppings, non-canned tomato juices, liquid essences, and preserved cherries. Benzoic acid also occurs naturally in some berries. It can cause gastric problems and may be a cause of food sensitivity in those suffering from asthma or urticaria.

BETA CAROTENE

Beta carotene is a naturally occurring yellow or orange pigment in plants, and is converted to vitamin A in the intestine. It is found in dark green leafy vegetables (cabbage, broccoli, lettuce, spinach), carrots, orange, mangoes, apricots, red capsicum (pepper) and tomatoes. Unlike vitamin A, it is not toxic if eaten in large quantities. However, hypercarotenaemia can occur if one regularly overconsumes foods rich in carotene. The skin develops an orange colour but will revert to normal colour once the diet returns to normal. Cases of hypercarotenaemia have occurred in women who eat large amounts of carrots.

BISCUITS

These are a popular snack food and bread alternative for both children and adults. Children love their crisp and crunchy texture. Biscuits are made from flour, fat, sugars and salt with various added ingredients and can be either sweet or savoury. Some sweet biscuits tend to be high in fat and have a high sugar content. However, plain sweet biscuit varieties (not chocolate coated) such as Milk Arrowroot, Milk Coffee, Shredded Wheatmeal, Marie and fruit-filled biscuits can make suitable snacks for children, as these biscuits are lower in fat and sugar than many other biscuits and commonly eaten snack foods such as cakes, muesli bars, doughnuts, chips, and chocolate. However, they still have the potential to cause tooth decay.

Savoury biscuits also vary in fat content but are much lower in sugar than sweet varieties. They tend to be high in salt, so choose low- or reduced-salt varieties where available. Savoury biscuits can make a healthy snack for children. Top with cheese, Vegemite, peanut butter, tomato.

BRAN

Bran refers to the outer layers of cereal grains. Once thrown out as a waste product of milling, it is now regarded as a valuable source of dietary fibre. Common brans are wheat, oats, barley and rice. Brans are useful for relieving constipation, and brans with a high soluble fibre content such as oats, barley and rice will also reduce cholesterol when a sufficient amount is taken. Bran supplements must be taken with plenty of water and exercise.

Bran supplements are not recommended for children as they can decrease the absorption of important minerals such as calcium, iron, zinc and magnesium and provide too much bulk so children have no 'room' for the more important nutritious foods they need for growth and development. Children will obtain all the fibre they need from wholegrain cereals and bread, fruits and vegetables, legumes and nuts without needing to resort to bran supplements.

BREAD

Bread is made from the basic ingredients: flour, salt, yeast and water. Other ingredients may include sugar, milk powder, vegetable oil, dry or wet gluten, yeast foods, bread improvers, dried fruits, eggs, cheese, spices and flavourings. All breads whether white, mixed-grain, wholemeal or rye are nutritious — supplying protein, complex carbohydrate (starch), dietary fibre, vitamins (particularly B group vitamins such as thiamine) and minerals (iron, calcium, zinc). Bread is a low-fat, low-sugar food and is moderate in energy: about 290 kilojoules (70 calories) per 30 g (1 oz) slice, the same as a piece of fruit. Dietary Guidelines recommend everyone eats more bread. Children 6–12 years need about 4–6 slices of bread a day.

BULIMIA NERVOSA

An eating disorder usually occurring in young girls and women to control their weight. It is characterised by an abnormal preoccupation with body shape and weight and involves periods of binge eating followed by vomiting. Unlike the anorexic, bulimics are usually of normal weight. It has been estimated that 1–2% of females of all ages experience some type of eating disorder, with bulimia being the commonest. It appears to be occurring at younger ages. One possible reason may be that parental preoccupation with weight and maintenance of thinness, is being passed onto children. A US study looking at 3000 young people aged 9–16 years found that 5% of the girls on one occasion had vomited to lose weight.

The physical effects of bulimia include loss of menstruation, infertility, stunted growth, 'feeling sick', osteoporosis, dental decay and loss of teeth. These can lead to kidney failure, muscle weakness and risk of heart problems. Psychological effects include depression, guilt, anger and shame about 'breaking the diet', bingeing and vomiting, irritability and withdrawing from friends. If you are concerned about bulimia talk to your doctor or dietitian.

BUTTER

Butter is made from cream which has been churned, causing water to separate and leaving a solid yellow mass. Salt is added for flavour and to enhance shelf life.

Butter contains 80% fat and 16% water and is a concentrated source of kilojoules (4040 kilojoules/740 calories per 100/3½ oz and 152 kilojoules/37 calories per teaspoon). It is a naturally good source of fat soluble vitamins A and D and supplies small amounts of vitamin E. Over the years the consumption of butter has fallen, not only because it is less spreadable than margarine but primarily because it is high in saturated fat and cholesterol, both contributors to heart disease. Butter contains 57% saturated fat (compared to 19% in polyunsaturated margarine and 15% in monounsaturated margarine), and has a cholesterol content of 200 mg per 100 g (3½ oz) and 10 mg per teaspoon. For those with a high cholesterol level or history of heart disease in the family it is advisable to use polyunsaturated or monounsaturated margarines. This also applies to children. However as with all fat spreads they should be used sparingly because of their high fat and kilojoule content.

Butter is also available in no-salt varieties, reduced-fat varieties (40% fat, half that of regular butter) and as dairy blend.

Dairy blend is made of a blend of milk fat and vegetable oil and has added vitamins A, D and salt, similar to butter. It was developed to produce a spread with the flavour of butter and the spreadability of margarine, but is still not suitable for those following cholesterol lowering diets.

Clarified butter or ghee is the purest form of butter with most of the milk solids and water removed and is popular in Indian cuisine.

CAFFEINE

Caffeine is a naturally occurring stimulant found in coffee, tea, cola beverages, cocoa and some drugs. Cola flavoured beverages have about 3 to 4 times less caffeine than tea or coffee.

Caffeine is rapidly absorbed by the body but does not accumulate, being excreted in the urine. Some of the effects of caffeine include wakefulness, relief from tiredness, and the need to 'wee' regularly.

Most of the caffeine in children's diets comes from a combination of tea, coffee and chocolate, with less than half from cola flavoured soft drinks. Although evidence of long-term detrimental effects from caffeine intake is lacking, there appears to be no benefits gained from caffeine consumption by children. As caffeine is a drug, some children may react adversely to it. To limit caffeine intake, restrict cocoa, chocolate, tea, coffee, and cola type drinks. Encourage water as the preferred drink.

CALCIUM

Calcium is an important mineral for the growth and development of teeth and bones, for the clotting of blood, for blood pressure and the proper functioning of nerves and muscles. The main sources are dairy foods such as milk, cheese and yoghurt. Some calcium is found in fish (with bones) such as sardines and salmon, and in vegetables such as broccoli, parsley, cabbage and legumes, almonds and oranges. While tofu (bean curd) is a good source of calcium, unfortified soy drink is not. Only soy drinks fortified with calcium — at least 120 mg of calcium per 100 ml ($3\frac{1}{2}$ fl oz) of milk — should be used for children. Skim milk and reduced-fat milks contain the same, if not slightly more calcium than whole cow's milk.

Calcium is especially important to prevent osteoporosis in later life. Lack of calcium in the primary and high school years can predispose one to osteoporosis, as this is the time when bone mass is increasing. (See also Cow's milk.)

CALORIES

The calorie is a measure of the quantity of energy that a food will provide. The metric term is the kilojoule. One calorie equals about 4 kilojoules. Although we speak of 'calories' the correct term is kilocalories or 1000 calories. Fats provide the most energy, at 9 calories or 37 kilojoules a gram, while protein and carbohydrate provide the least: 4 calories or 16–17 kilojoules a gram. In most Western countries too much food energy is derived from fats. Most of our energy should come from carbohydrates.

CANNED FOODS

Canning is a process whereby foods are preserved to ensure year round availability and variety. The basic steps in canning include preparation of the product, filling into a can and closing, sterilization by heating to destroy bacteria and finally cooling. Recent studies have confirmed that canned foods are similar in nutritional value to their fresh counterparts. No preservatives are used in canned foods as the process itself is the preservative.

CARBOHYDRATES

Carbohydrates provide energy for the body. There are two types of carbohydrates: simple and complex. Simple carbohydrates are sugars such as glucose, fructose (fruit sugar), galactose, maltose, sucrose and lactose. Complex carbohydrates are starches. Glucose is the main fuel for the brain, and most sugars and starches are ultimately converted into glucose by the body. Most fruits, vegetables, cereals, breads, legumes and nuts contain a mixture of simple sugars and complex carbohydrates. Most sugars are found in fruits and vegetables, sugar cane, milk, breads, honey and jam. Complex carbohydrates are found in bread, cereals, fruits, vegetables and legumes. Carbohydrates contain only half the energy of fats. Health authorities recommend that the bulk of our diet comes from carbohydrates.

Latest research shows that the old idea of carbohydrates being fattening is false. In fact, carbohydrates can actually help weight loss as the conversion of carbohydrates to fat doesn't play a major role in the production and storage of body fat. An increase in body fat comes from eating fat containing foods. So eat low-fat carbohydrate foods such as bread, cereals, pasta, rice, fruit and vegetables. Eat them plain or serve with reduced-fat spreads, milks and sauces.

CHOLESTEROL

Cholesterol is a fatty white substance made in the liver. It is essential for health, being an important part of the membranes of the brain and nerves, and is needed for the production of certain hormones and vitamin D.

Cholesterol rich foods include those of animal origin such as meat, eggs, dairy foods, poultry. It is not found in plant foods. Eating high cholesterol foods alone will not raise cholesterol. A high cholesterol level is a result of the liver overproducing cholesterol together with a diet high in saturated fat.

Two important types of cholesterol are LDL and HDL. HDL is the 'good cholesterol'. It protects against cholesterol build up and therefore heart disease. LDL is the 'bad cholesterol' and gets clogged up in arteries and veins. Recent surveys have shown that large numbers of primary school children have high cholesterol levels and this is of concern. This may be a result of a high saturated fat intake from snack and convenience foods. To avoid a high cholesterol, eat a diet low in fat, particularly saturated fat, and a diet high in dietary fibre such as wholegrain cereals and bread, fruits, vegetables, nuts and legumes. Use polyunsaturated or monounsaturated margarines or oils and lean meats.

Children should not be given a low-fat, low-cholesterol diet without the supervision of a dietitian or doctor, as nutrients required for growth and development may be excluded. Children from families with a history of high cholesterol and heart disease will need dietary assessment and advice.

COELIAC DISEASE

This is a lifelong dietary intolerance to gluten, the protein in wheat, rye, triticale, oats and barley which causes damage to the lining of the small intestine so that food is not absorbed properly and nutrient deficiencies occur. Diarrhoea, weight loss, nausea, wind, tiredness, abdominal discomfort and poor growth are common complaints. Removal of gluten from the diet returns the small intestine to normal and symptoms disappear. Coeliac disease affects about 1 person in 2000 or 3000. It tends to run in families, with about 1 in 10 close family relatives of an affected person also possibly having the disease. Contact your doctor if coeliac disease is suspected and your local branch of the Coeliac Society.

COLOURINGS

Colourings are added to some foods to improve their appearance. Only colours allowed in Government Food Standards Codes can be added to foods which are permitted to contain them. Colours can be natural or synthetic. Concern about the use of colours arises from a safety issue and the fact that certain colours (e.g. tartrazine, blue, green and red colours) can cause unpleasant reactions in sensitive individuals. Colours, if used, are listed in ingredient lists on food labels. (See also Additives, food.)

CONSTIPATION

Constipation refers to the consistency or hardness of the 'poo' rather than the frequency. Some of the causes of constipation include a diet lacking in fibre, lack of exercise and water, emotional stress such as starting at a new school, family problems and children ignoring nature's call because they are too busy playing. To prevent constipation, include high-fibre foods and water in the diet, add stewed prunes to breakfast cereal or dessert or use prune juice, encourage exercise, and encourage your child to go to the toilet when he needs to. Soft liquorice, an old fashioned remedy for constipation, works wonders when all else fails. If constipation continues to be a problem, see your doctor. (See also Fibre.)

COW'S MILK

This is an important food for all children being the most important source of calcium in their diet and a major source of B vitamins (particularly riboflavin, vitamin B12), protein, vitamin A, zinc and energy.

Children 6–12 years need a minimum of 700 ml (24 fl oz) of milk a day.

If your child does not drink cow's milk, the same nutrients will be found in other dairy foods; for example, about 3 cups (700 ml/24 fl oz) of cow's milk is equivalent nutritionally to about 1 cup (250 ml/8 fl oz) of milk plus a tub of yoghurt and a slice of cheese. From 5 years reduced-fat milks can be used for children, provided the child is eating a well-rounded diet. Skim milk is not generally liked by children, and is also lower in fat soluble vitamins and energy than reduced-fat milk.

If children do not take any cow's milk or other dairy products their calcium intake will be low. A calcium-fortified soy beverage — with at least 120 mg of calcium per 100 ml (3½ fl oz) of milk — or calcium supplements will be required. See your dietitian or doctor. Low calcium intake in childhood can lead to osteoporosis in later life. (See also Calcium.)

COW'S MILK ALLERGY

This allergy is a reaction to the protein in cow's milk. While many people may believe they have an allergy to cow's milk, in reality it affects only about 3–5% of the population. Soy and goat's milk are not suitable substitute milks, as in many cases those with cow's milk allergy also have an allergy to goat's- and soy-milk proteins. Consult with your doctor or dietitian.

Many people claim that their allergy to milk causes mucus (i.e. coughs or congestion). Numerous studies have failed to show an association between milk and the symptoms of mucus production in healthy young people. It appears that the physical effects are not caused solely or specifically by milk.

Most children tend to grow out of their allergies, so cow's milk should be reintroduced into the diet after a period of time, to see whether symptoms are still present or are now absent.

CYSTIC FIBROSIS

This is a genetically inherited disease involving the pancreas, lung, bowel, liver and sweat glands. It occurs in about 1 in every 2000 live births. The pancreas fails to produce the enzyme to digest fats, and enzyme supplements must be given. Respiratory problems are also a common feature. Specialized diets are required to ensure energy and levels of nutrients remain high for growth and development. Children with cystic fibrosis should be seen by a doctor and dietitian. All newborn infants are screened for cystic fibrosis at birth.

DEHYDRATION

Dehydration is loss of water from the body so severe that essential functions can't be performed. Dehydration can cause death and usually results from diarrhoea and vomiting. Signs of dehydration include weight loss, thirst, lethargy, sunken eyes, low blood pressure, little or no urine output, pinched skin retracts slowly or very slowly. Children need about 1000–1500 ml (32–48 fl oz) of water daily.

Always check with your doctor if your child has difficulty or is unable to take any fluids or if you suspect your child may become dehydrated.

DENTAL HEALTH
See Chapter Four.

DEXTRINS

Dextrins are chains of glucose formed by the breakdown of starch during digestion and when starch is heated. They are also used in food as a thickening agent.

DIARRHOEA

Diarrhoea is the frequent passing of very loose 'poos' and is often associated with vomiting and tummy pains. It can be caused by bacteria (such as in food poisoning), viruses (as in gastroenteritis), infections of the urinary and respiratory tract, antibiotics and some medical conditions such as diabetes, coeliac disease and cystic fibrosis. Diarrhoea is the body's way of getting rid of an offending toxin, and in the process water and important body minerals or electrolytes are lost. Loss of too much water and minerals can cause death. Always consult your doctor for the appropriate treatment of diarrhoea.

The aim of treating diarrhoea is to prevent dehydration. Always make sure that your hands, clothes and work areas are clean.

For children with diarrhoea who are not dehydrated, stop food for the first 12–24 hours and give clear fluids only. Suitable fluids include:

- Electrolyte solutions (follow manufacturer's directions).
- Cordials (not low-joule, diluted 1 in 6 with tap water).
- Flat carbonated drinks (not low-joule), unsweetened fruit juice, fruit juice drinks (diluted 1 in 4 with tap water).
- Glucose (2 teaspoons in 240 ml/8 fl oz boiled water).

Always dilute sugared drinks as the sugar can exacerbate the diarrhoea.

Food should be introduced within 24 hours even if diarrhoea has not settled.

Foods which are well-tolerated include potato, pasta, rice, noodles, vegetables, biscuits, bread, toast, meat, eggs, fish and soup (not milk).

Milk products, sugary foods (jelly, honey, jam) dried fruits and fruit should be avoided for a few days as they may exacerbate the diarrhoea. In some cases when milk is reintroduced, diarrhoea may restart or worsen. This may be due to a temporary inability to handle milk sugar (lactose) and a suitable low-lactose milk may be necessary.

Some diarrhoea occurs when children drink too much fruit juice or eat too much fruit, particularly those varieties with high fructose content such as apples, prunes and pears. Artificially sweetened drinks with sorbitol may also cause diarrhoea as will a diet that is low in fat. Check that your child is having a well-rounded intake of food and is not drinking too much juice nor eating too many sugary foods.

DIETARY GUIDELINES

Dietary Guidelines have been formulated by health authorities to promote wellness in the community and to reduce the risk of diet-related diseases such as heart disease, obesity, diabetes and cancer. As adult Dietary Guidelines are not directly applicable to children, Draft Dietary Guidelines for Australian children have been proposed. These are as follows:

- Encourage and support breast feeding.
- Children need enough food and appropriate physical activity to grow and develop normally; growth should be checked regularly.
- Enjoy a wide variety of nutritious foods.
- Eat plenty of breads, cereals, vegetables (including legumes) and fruits.

- Low-fat diets are not suitable for young children, but for older children a diet low in fat and in particular, low in saturated fat is appropriate.
- Water is encouraged as a drink for children; alcohol is not recommended.
- Eat only moderate amounts of sugars and foods containing added sugars.
- Choose low-salt foods and use salt sparingly.
- Guidelines on specific nutrients: eat food containing calcium; eat food containing iron.

DIGESTION

Digestion is the process by which food is broken down so that the nutrients can be used by the body. The mouth, stomach, pancreas, liver and intestine produce juices and enzymes to break food down. Proteins are converted to amino acids, carbohydrates to glucose and fructose and fats to fatty acids and glycerol.

DISACCHARIDES

Disaccharides are sugars made up of two simple sugars such as lactose (glucose and galactose), sucrose (glucose and fructose) and maltose (glucose and glucose). They must be broken down by enzymes in the digestive system to their single sugars (or monosaccharides) before being absorbed and used for energy.

ELECTROLYTES

These include the minerals sodium, potassium, calcium, chloride, magnesium and phosphorous. They influence the water distribution and balance within body cells. Disturbance of electrolyte balance can occur from sweating, diarrhoea and vomiting. Water is usually lost before electrolytes so it is important to replace fluid rather than electrolytes in the first instance, particularly after sweating.

ENERGY

Energy is the ability to do work. It is needed by the body for physical activity, to maintain body temperature, for metabolism and growth. Energy comes from the breakdown of foods and is measured in kilojoules or calories. (See also Calories.)

EGGS

Eggs are nutritious foods containing protein, fat, vitamins A, B, D, E and the minerals calcium, phosphorous, zinc and iron, although the iron is poorly absorbed. One egg contains about 355 kilojoules (85 calories). The missing nutrients are fibre and vitamin C.

Eggs have been criticized because of their high cholesterol content. However, recent research has shown that eating one or two eggs a day will not increase blood cholesterol. So let your child enjoy an egg or two a day.

FAST FOODS

A term used to describe foods that are convenient, require little if any cooking and little chewing. They tend to be high in fat, kilojoules/calories, salt and lack fibre. Examples include pies, sausage rolls, chips, fried chicken, hamburgers, pizza, battered fish. Some fast foods are nutritionally better than others.

FAT CHILDREN

About 20–30% of Australian children are estimated to be overweight, and indications are that they are getting fatter. This is a concern as fat children often suffer emotional stress, unhappiness and teasing by their peers which can affect their personality as well as lead to health problems later in life. Being overweight or fat also places physical limits on the child's ability to participate in sports, and places them at higher risk of being overweight as an adult.

Children become fat when their food intake is greater than their needs for physical activity and growth. Prevention is better than cure, so ensure your child and the rest of the family eats sensibly. Avoid high-fat and high-sugar snacks and encourage exercise.

Keep these important points in mind:

- It's not always possible to tell whether a child is overweight just by looking at him. Before jumping to conclusions and labelling your child 'fat' see your dietitian or doctor so your child's weight can be checked against his height for his age to ensure that he is in proportion and growing normally. Your dietitian or doctor will have special height–weight references for children (adult height–weight references are unsuitable). Remember that during puberty great physical changes take place, which may be interpreted incorrectly as 'getting fat'.

- Not all fat children eat more than normal weight children. Research indicates that hereditary plays a part and that some fat children may inherit genes that make them good storers of fat. It is estimated that if one parent is obese, the likelihood of the child being overweight as an adult is about 40%, if two parents are obese the likelihood is 80%.

- Overweight between 6 and 11 years is a good indicator as to whether your child will be overweight as an adolescent or adult.

- Don't put your child on a diet, as this may affect growth and lead to emotional and psychological trauma. Encourage sensible eating for the whole family and exercise. Aim to maintain the child's present weight and prevent weight gain. As the child grows he will fall into the ideal height and weight range.

- Don't overemphasise diet and fatness to your child as a negative trait as it could lead to anorexia or bulimia to control weight in later years.

- Set a good example with family eating habits. Do not have lollies, chocolates, cakes or chips in the house, as these will tempt the child. An overweight child will 'grow into' a healthy weight range more easily if the family gives support and encouragement by following the same healthy eating plan as the overweight child. However, to encourage normality and compliance with good eating, allow some treat foods in small serves on special occasions when others are having them.

FATS

Fats are an important energy source, containing twice the kilojoules/calories of carbohydrate and protein. Fats are important for growth, for brain and nervous tissue, for fat soluble vitamins and cholesterol. Very low-fat diets are not recommended for children as it is difficult for them to obtain their energy requirements for growth and development without fat. Whereas adults are advised to obtain only 30% of their energy from fats, children in the age range 5–12 years need at least 35% of their energy from fat. Poor fat intake with an excessive intake of fruit, fruit juice and sugary foods can lead to diarrhoea. However, children should be encouraged to exercise moderation with regard to their use of fat, by trimming fat from meat; using only small amounts of butter, margarine, oils, gravies, cream; and limiting fried foods, chips, fatty snack foods to only occasional use.

A high-fat intake (from high-fat snack foods, fried foods, oils, margarine, chocolates) together with little exercise is a major cause of overweight in children, as fat eaten is stored as fat in the body.

FATTY ACIDS

Fats are made up of fatty acids and glycerol and are usually described by their predominant fatty acid content which can be either saturated or unsaturated. Unsaturated fatty acids are either monounsaturated or polyunsaturated. Most fats are a mixture of all three fatty acids. Saturated fats are hard fats at room temperature and contain no double bonds in their structure. Monounsaturated and polyunsaturated fats (unsaturated fats) are either soft fats or liquid at room temperature. Monounsaturated fats contain only one double bond while polyunsaturated fats contain two or more double bonds. Monounsaturated and polyunsaturated fats help reduce the risk of heart disease.

Trans fatty acids are also unsaturated fatty acids and are found naturally in the fats of beef, lamb and dairy products. They are formed during the manufacture of some shortenings and margarines when vegetable oils are hardened to make them spreadable. Trans fatty acids, like saturated fats, raise cholesterol levels and so are a risk factor for heart disease. While polyunsaturated and monounsaturated margarines contain some trans fatty acids, they are still a healthier choice than butter, because their total content of saturated and trans fatty acids is much lower.

FIBRE

Fibre is undigested plant food which escapes digestion in the small intestine but which is fermented by bacteria in the lower bowel. It is found in fruits, vegetables, cereals (breakfast cereals, grains, rice, pasta), bread, legumes and nuts but is not found in animal food. Fibre prevents constipation, slows the rate of digestion and gives a feeling of 'fullness' and may protect against overweight, bowel cancer and heart disease.

There are two types of fibre — soluble and insoluble. Soluble fibre is found in fruits, vegetables, legumes, rice, barley, psyllium and oats and is useful in lowering cholesterol. It also helps to prevent and relieve constipation but not to the same degree as insoluble fibre. Insoluble fibre is found in wheat bran and wheat based foods and is very effective in preventing and relieving constipation.

Diets too high in fibre are not recommended for children. Children tend to have limited 'stomach capacity' and, because fibre is filling, too much fibre can prevent their eating enough food that is needed for energy, growth and development. Fibre can also adversely affect the absorption of certain important minerals.

While it is recommended that adults take at least 25–30 g (1 oz) fibre per day, this is probably too high for children. Recent recommendations from the American Health Foundation suggest an 'age plus five' amount. A six year old would therefore need 11 g (⅓ oz) of fibre a day and a 12 year old 17 g (½ oz) a day, which is about half the adult requirement.

Children should obtain fibre from a variety of fibre sources and not bran supplements. Water and exercise should be encouraged to gain the benefits of fibre. (See also Bran.)

FLUORIDE
See Chapter Four.

FOOD INTOLERANCE
This is often confused with food allergy. Food intolerance does not involve the immune system nor is it a reaction to a protein. It is a reaction to the various added or natural chemicals in foods. The chemicals involved include salicylates (found in fruits, vegetables, nuts, herbs, honey, spices, juices, jams, peppermint); amines (cheese, chocolate, fish, yeast extracts, bananas, avocados); MSG (cheese, stock cubes, sauces, meat extracts, and which occurs naturally in tomatoes and mushrooms); food additives such as tartrazine (the yellow colour used in jelly, custard powder) and sulphites (the preservative in dried fruit, sausages, commercial fresh fruit salad, wine). Symptoms are similar to an adverse drug reaction and include tiredness, tummy pains, diarrhoea, headache and hives. Children usually become irritable and restless.

Food intolerance is difficult to diagnose as it usually involves more than one food and reactions are not immediate but occur hours later. See your doctor or dietitian if you suspect a food intolerance.

FRUCTOSE
Fructose is often referred to as fruit sugar because it is mainly found in fruit such as apples, bananas, cherries, figs, grapes, pears, plums and prunes. It is also the primary sugar in honey. Fructose is about one-and-a-half times as sweet as sucrose (table sugar) and does not require insulin for its absorption. Because it is not completely absorbed by young children it can cause diarrhoea, wind and bloating.

FRUIT JUICES

Fruit juices are sources of vitamin C with small amounts of other vitamins and minerals. They contain little fat and dietary fibre, being predominantly carbohydrate.

Commercial fruit juices by law must contain 100% fruit juice. Fruit juice drinks contain 25–50% juice, and fruit drinks 5–25% juice. All commercial juices contain added vitamin C.

Overconsumption of fruit juice is a common problem in children, often leading to stomach cramps and diarrhoea. Limit juice to one serve per day and encourage water as the main fluid. Eat fruit in preference to juice to obtain important nutrients and fibre.

GALACTOSE

Galactose is a sugar which in combination with glucose, forms lactose the sugar of milk. It is also found in the dietary fibres pectin and galactomannan and some fruits and vegetables. In the liver it is broken down to glucose. Children can be born with galactosemia, an error of metabolism where the liver cannot break down galactose to glucose.

GASTROENTERITIS

A life threatening viral infection of the stomach and intestine causing diarrhoea, vomiting and tummy pains. (See also Dehydration, Diarrhoea.)

GLUCOSE

Glucose is the most important sugar in the body, being a major source of energy for the brain and nervous tissue and the form in which carbohydrate is circulated in the blood. Starch and sugars (with the exception of fructose) are broken down to glucose before absorption.

GLUTEN

Gluten is a complex protein found predominantly in wheat but also in smaller amount in rye, triticale, oats and barley. It is the gluten protein in wheat flour which gives bread its structure, strength and ability to rise. Gluten is also used as a binder in sausages, small goods and pet foods. Children and adults with coeliac disease must avoid foods containing gluten. (See also Coeliac disease.)

GUMS

Gums are polysaccharides naturally found in plants and form part of dietary fibre. In foods they are used as thickeners and for texture. Gums cause a slow rise in blood sugar as they are broken down slowly. They also help prevent constipation.

HEALTH FOODS

Health foods is a general term used to describe foods which are not processed or which have undergone little processing or are grown without the use of chemical herbicides and pesticides (e.g. 'unprocessed', 'natural', 'organic'). They are said to be better for you than regular foods but in most cases offer no real benefits (e.g. honey versus sugar; raw sugar versus white; so-called 'health bars' versus chocolate).

HERBAL TEAS

These teas are made from a mixture of leaves, flowers, roots, stems and bark of various herbs and shrubs. They should be used with caution in children because they may contain naturally present toxic substances and be questionable in terms of their hygiene and safety. Herbal teas are no healthier than regular tea. While most don't contain caffeine, some do have tannins (e.g. teas made from Blackberry, Peppermint, Lady's Mantle and Uva-ursi). If using herbal teas, make them weak and buy only packaged varieties with an ingredient list rather than buying them loose from a market stall.

HONEY

Honey is a sweet syrup produced from the nectar of flowers. It contains 75% sugars and 25% water and has no fat or protein. Honey is often used as a sugar substitute in the belief that it has more nutrients. While it does contain nutrients such as calcium, iron and zinc these are in such small amounts that their contribution to the diet is negligible. Honey, as with all sugars, can cause tooth decay.

HUNGER

A feeling of emptiness in the stomach when food from the previous meal has been digested and absorbed. Blood sugar levels drop and the brain signals the stomach to contract.

HYPERACTIVITY

A term used to describe children that have short attention span, poor concentration, are hard to discipline, uncoordinated, throw tantrums, have unpredictable behaviours and generally can't control themselves.

Much controversy has surrounded the link between diet and hyperactivity. Dr Ben Feingold claimed a dramatic improvement in 50% of children when salicylates, artificial colours and flavours were eliminated from the diet. The Feingold diet has been widely challenged and criticized and largely disproved. Despite this, various food sensitivities have been found in some hyperactive children.

Research linking hyperactivity to refined sugar foods has also been disproved. Recent work indicates a link in between low iron levels (and subsequent anaemia) in infancy and hyperactivity. Iron is important for the proper growth and development of the brain. A lack of iron means less oxygen reaches the brain. Iron may have an independent role in the formation, function and breakdown of the brain's messenger substances.

HYPOGLYCAEMIA

Refers to a low blood sugar level. It is caused by an overproduction of insulin, which moves sugar out of the blood into the cells. Severe cases occur in diabetics. Symptoms include dizziness, shaking, sweating, confusion and, in the case of diabetics, can lead to a coma. Cases of true hypoglycaemia, other than in diabetics, are rare. Some people feel weak if they haven't eaten for a while but usually their sugar levels are normal. Having small, regular meals will solve the problem.

IODINE

Iodine is required for growth and for the thyroid gland to make thyroxine, which controls the body's metabolism. It is found in iodized salt, seafood and dairy products.

The amount of iodine in food depends on the iodine content of the area where the the food or raw materials were grown. Lack of iodine can lead to goitre. It is toxic in large doses.

IRON

Iron is an important mineral, necessary for growth and brain development. It forms the main part of haemoglobin, which carries oxygen in the blood. It is also important in muscles, as myoglobin, where it provides oxygen for physical activity. Research is showing that many children are not getting enough iron to meet their requirements.

The best sources of iron are from animal foods such as beef, lamb, pork, chicken and fish, which contain haem iron. Children should be encouraged to have some meat in their diet.

Plant foods contain non-haem iron which is not as well-absorbed. Non-haem iron sources are legumes, breads, breakfast cereals, rice, pasta, fruits and vegetables. However, the absorption of iron from plant sources can be enhanced by eating them with a vitamin C rich food (e.g. fruit on breakfast cereal; orange juice and toast) or eating them with meat (e.g. steak and vegetables).

While cow's milk and eggs are from an animal source, their iron is not haem iron and so is less available. In fact cow's milk can inhibit the absorption of iron from foods, so don't always serve milk as the beverage at mealtimes! (See also Anaemia.)

JUICE

See Fruit juices.

JUNK FOOD

The term 'junk food' is used to describe foods that are generally very high in fat, high in sugar, high in salt and high in kilojoules/calories but contain very few of the essential vitamins and minerals. It is often used when talking about takeaway foods, confectionery and soft drinks. It is a term that is used loosely and, unfortunately, not always justified.

K, VITAMIN

Is a fat soluble vitamin found mainly in green vegetables, liver and soy beans. It is also made by the bacteria in the intestine. Vitamin K's main function is for blood clotting.

Newborn babies are given an injection or oral dose of vitamin K at birth, as their intestines are free of the bacteria that make vitamin K and their stores limited. This prevents the risk of haemorrhage and bleeding in the newborn.

KILOJOULE

Is the measure of the energy content of a food. (See also Energy, Calories.)

LACTOSE

Lactose is commonly called the sugar of milk. Lactose is broken down to glucose and galactose by the enzyme lactase found in the small intestine. Lactose is found in all types of milk (being higher in reduced- and low-fat milks than whole milk), yoghurt, ice-cream and commercial foods containing dairy products. It is not found in hard cheese or soy beverages. Lactose is the least sweet of all the sugars.

LACTOSE INTOLERANCE

Lactose intolerance is a condition in which lactose is not broken down to its component sugars (glucose and galactose) due to the presence of only small amounts of the lactase enzyme or a complete absence of lactase. About 70% of the world's population has difficulty digesting lactose. The incidence is low for Caucasian populations in Australia, New Zealand, North America and Europe but is higher in Chinese, Indian, Japanese, Arabic, Samoan, Maori and black Australian and American populations, who have a genetic predisposition to lactase deficiency. In these groups the lactase enzyme starts to disappear after about 3 years of age so they can only take small amounts of dairy products. Lactose intolerance also occurs temporarily after gastroenteritis and in association with some medical conditions such as AIDS/HIV and coeliac disease.

Symptoms of lactose intolerance include watery and explosive diarrhoea, tummy pains and wind. In children with a genetic predisposition to lactose intolerance it could be one of the causes of tummy pains and wind.

Treatment involves removal or restriction of dairy products and foods containing dairy products and lactose from the diet. As dairy products are a major source of calcium in a child's diet, a milk substitute must be given. Calcium-fortified soy beverages are suitable. See your doctor or dietitian if lactose intolerance is suspected or for dietary advice.

LAXATIVES

Laxatives are used by adults to relieve constipation and may contain bulking agents such as gums or chemicals which affect the wall of the bowel. Laxatives are not recommended for use by children for constipation except on the advice of a doctor. They can cause uncomfortable tummy pains, loss of water and a general weak feeing. (See also Constipation.)

LEGUMES

Legumes are a tasty, economical source of protein, complex carbohydrate, dietary fibre, vitamins and minerals. They are also low in fat.

Legumes include all dried peas and haricot, lima, kidney, navy, soy beans and lentils. Baked beans are made from navy beans and are an excellent and well-liked substitute for meat in children's diets.

All beans (except ready prepared canned beans) need to be soaked before cooking and bought to the rapid boil for 5–10 minutes to kill any toxins present in the legumes. (See also Baked beans.)

LINOLEIC ACID

This is an essential polyunsaturated fatty acid and belongs to the omega 6 series of fatty acids. It plays an important role in the body, particularly with regard to its protective effect against heart disease. It removes some of the undesirable fats from the blood circulation so they do not clog arteries or veins.

Linoleic acid is found in polyunsaturated vegetable oils and margarines (sunflower, safflower, corn), walnuts, brazil nuts, peanut butter and peanuts. Small amounts are found in chicken, egg, beef and grains.

LINOLENIC ACID

This is a polyunsaturated fatty acid. Alpha linolenic acid is an omega 3 fatty acid which is converted in the body to eicosapentaenoic acid (EPA) and docosahexanoic acid (DHA), important for the eyes, brain and nervous tissue as well as for the formation of prostaglandins. It is found in certain fish, the leaves of plants, linseed and walnuts. (See also Omega 3 fatty acids.)

LOW-FAT DIETS

See Fats, Cow's milk.

LOW-FAT AND REDUCED-FAT MILKS

See Cow's milk.

MANNITOL

A sweetening substitute used in some low-joule jellies, jams, drinks and chocolate. It is about as sweet as glucose but contributes only half the kilojoules, as a large proportion is not absorbed. Too much mannitol can cause diarrhoea.

MICROWAVE COOKING

Microwave cooking is a quick and efficient way of heating foods with minimal loss of nutrients, providing cooking times are right. It involves the use of high energy radiation which heats the water particles within foods, so it is similar to steaming or boiling. Microwaves heat food from the outside in, so it is important to stir before serving. Foods continue to cook once removed from the microwave oven.

MINERALS

There are at least 20 different minerals needed for health. They are important for building healthy bones and teeth, for forming parts of important body compounds such as haemoglobin and myoglobin, and in solution for maintaining fluid balance. Important minerals for growth and development include calcium, phosphorous, iron, sodium, potassium, zinc, magnesium, sulphur and chlorine. Trace minerals required in small amounts include chromium, iodine, selenium, silicon, fluorine and manganese.

Minerals most at risk for children include iron, calcium and zinc.

MONOUNSATURATED FATTY ACIDS

These are found in olives and olive oil, canola (rapeseed) oil, sunola oil, avocados, lean beef, lean pork, veal, chicken, salmon, tuna, almonds, peanuts, peanut oil and peanut butter.

They are protective against heart disease, they lower cholesterol and have a beneficial effect on blood pressure. They are more suitable for frying than polyunsaturated fat, as they do not oxidise or smoke as quickly at high temperatures.

MONOSACCHARIDES

Monosaccharides are single, simple sugars — such as glucose, fructose and galactose — that don't need to be further digested before being absorbed by the body.

MSG (MONOSODIUM GLUTAMATE)

MSG is the sodium salt of glutamic acid, an amino acid which is an important component of proteins. Glutamate (the salt of glutamic acid) is naturally present in many foods such as meat, fish, breast milk, cow's milk, Parmesan cheese and vegetables (spinach, corn, peas, tomatoes and carrots). The brain, muscles and other organs of the body also contain glutamate.

MSG is used as a flavour enhancer in many foods (soups, sauces and stock cubes).

Some individuals are sensitive to MSG. However reactions are rarely due to MSG alone but occur in combination with a sensitivity to other food chemicals such as salicylates and amines. The reaction occurs when a particular dose is exceeded.

A well-known case of MSG sensitivity is the 'Chinese Restaurant Syndrome'. This is characterised by headaches, tightness or numbness and sensations of burning in the face, neck and chest. It is interesting to note that surveys have shown that the glutamate content of Italian meals is much higher than Chinese meals!

Extensive research worldwide has demonstrated that MSG is safe for human consumption.

NIACIN (NICOTINIC ACID)

Also known as vitamin B3, niacin is a B group vitamin concerned with the release of energy from foods. It is important in nerve cells, effective in large doses in lowering cholesterol, and is involved in the production of some fatty acids. Niacin can be made from the amino acid tryptophan. Sources include liver, bread, wholegrain cereals, peanut butter, lean meats, yeast extracts, milk and eggs.

NOODLES

Noodles are a traditional staple food of China, Japan and South East Asia and are now popular foods in Western countries. They are made from cereal grains, such as wheat and rice. Pasta and noodles are often referred to as being the same, but in reality both differ in their origin, raw materials and method of manufacture. Pasta is the term for the Italian-style extruded products, such as macaroni and spaghetti, which are made from coarse semolina milled from hard wheats. Noodles, on the other hand, are Asian in origin and are made from bread wheat flour of a finer particle size than semolina by a process of sheeting and cutting. Noodles are useful nutritionally, being high in complex carbohydrate (starch) and low in fat. Noodles are sold dried or fresh, and are served with vegetables, meats and sauces.

The most popular type of noodle in Western countries is instant noodles. They are usually made from wheat flour and are steamed and fried in vegetable oil (palm oil) after cutting. The noodles are wrapped and sold with a sachet containing a flavouring concentrate. They cook quickly, in about 2–3 minutes, in boiling water. However, unlike traditional dried and fresh noodles, they are much higher in fat, about 17–20%. The flavouring concentrate is also very high in salt.

NUTRASWEET

Nutrasweet is the brand name for the sugar substitute aspartame. (See Aspartame.)

NUTS

Nuts are edible seeds which are found within a hard outer shell. They are nutritious foods, being a useful source of protein (7–20%), dietary fibre, vitamins (particularly E and B), and minerals such as iron, calcium, zinc, magnesium, potassium and phosphorous. They are high in fat, ranging from 36% in hazelnuts and coconut to 75% in macadamias. With the exception of coconut and palm nuts, the fats are either predominantly polyunsaturated or monounsaturated. Nuts contain no cholesterol and are low in carbohydrate. They can be processed into flours and pastes. Peanut butter is a nutritious and well-liked spread for children.

OATS

Oats are a popular cereal grain and require some processing before consumption. They are sold as rolled oats, oat bran and oatmeal and are a popular ingredient in bread, biscuits, breakfast cereal and cakes. They have the highest fat content of all the cereal grains, at 7%. This is predominantly polyunsaturated and monounsaturated. Oats are also a good source of complex carbohydrate (starch) and dietary fibre, B vitamins, calcium and iron. Because they contain gluten protein they are not suitable for those with coeliac disease.

OBESITY

Is the more extreme form of overweight. A child is said to be obese when his weight is 20% more than the average weight for his height. Average weight is based on height–weight tables. Apart from obesity being a risk to physical health, psychological problems are associated with obesity as children are often teased by their peers. Much of the overweight and obesity in children today is a result of lack of physical activity rather than an increase in food intake. Obesity can be prevented by encouraging good eating habits and exercise. (See also Fat children.)

OLIVE OIL
Is a popular oil used in Mediterranean cooking. It is very high in monounsaturated fatty acids, which are protective against heart disease. Like all oils, it is a concentrated source of energy (kilojoules/calories).

OMEGA 3 FATTY ACIDS
These are derived from the polyunsaturated fatty acid linolenic acid. Sources include breast milk, fish (salmon, tuna, mackerel, herring, sardines), egg yolk, lean red meats, pork, canola oil, walnuts and soy beans. They are protective against heart disease and stroke; increase bleeding time, so protect against thrombosis; lower blood pressure; may improve arthritis; and may be important in cancer and asthma prevention.

PALM OIL
Palm oil is a vegetable oil popularly used in processed foods such as biscuits, snack foods, cakes and bread. There are two types of palm oil — palm kernel oil and palm oil. Palm kernel oil is an expensive oil, contains 86% saturated fat, and is rarely used in processed foods. Palm oil is a cheaper oil and is the most common vegetable oil used in processed foods because of its physical and chemical properties. Unlike palm kernel oil, palm oil contains only 50% saturated fat with the remainder being monounsaturated (39%) and polyunsaturated (11%) fat. Palm oil contains no trans fatty acids. There is controversy surrounding the nutritional effects of palm oil, but it is generally not recommended for those with high cholesterol or at risk from heart disease.

PASTA
Pasta is a favourite with children. It is made from wheat semolina and is a rich source of complex carbohydrate (starch). Pasta is Italian in origin and includes spaghetti and macaroni. It is a low-fat food when eaten on its own, and supplies protein, vitamins and minerals. Traditionally it is eaten with vegetable and meat or cheese sauces.

PECTIN
Pectin is a soluble fibre, found in citrus peel and other fruits and vegetables. It is important for making jams and marmalades as it helps them to set. It is also used as a thickening agent in almond paste, fruit-flavoured fillings and spreads, confectionery, chutneys, sauces, salad dressings and mayonnaises. In the body it delays emptying of the stomach and helps to lower cholesterol.

PHENYLKETONURIA (PKU)
PKU is a genetically inherited disease in which the body can't metabolize the amino acid phenylalanine due to a deficiency of the enzyme to break it down (phenylalanine hydroxylase). It is rare, occurring in about 1 in 11 000 births. All babies are screened at birth for PKU in

Australia, USA and other countries. If it is not detected, phenylalanine levels rise too high and lead to retardation. Dietary restriction must be commenced from birth. The sugar substitute aspartame is not recommended for those with PKU.

PHOSPHOROUS
Phosphorous is needed for bones and teeth, and for the body to use proteins, fats, carbohydrates and some B group vitamins efficiently. Sources include lean meat, chicken, fish, eggs, milk, breast milk, cheese, bran, wholegrain cereals, legumes and nuts.

PHYTATES
Phytates are compounds found in the outer layers of cereal grains which can bind with important minerals such as iron, calcium, magnesium, zinc and make them unavailable to the body. Too much phytate can be a problem when large quantities of wheat bran supplements are given. Generally phytates in bread are broken down during fermentation so are not a problem.

POLYUNSATURATED FATS
These fats are found in polyunsaturated oils and margarines (sunflower, safflower, maize, cottonseed), soya beans, fish, walnuts and brazil nuts. They are protective against heart disease as they lower cholesterol levels.

POTASSIUM
Potassium is needed to regulate the amount of fluid inside and outside the cells, helps nerves and muscles to function properly and to offer protection against too much sodium in the diet. It is found in vegetables,

fruit (fresh and dried), milk, fish, meat, nuts, wholegrain cereals and bread.

Vomiting and diarrhoea are usually associated with a loss of potassium.

P:S RATIO
All fats are a mixture of saturated, polyunsaturated and monounsaturated fats. The P:S ratio is the ratio of polyunsaturated fat to saturated fat in a food. For example the P:S ratio of polyunsaturated margarines is 2:1, that is, there is twice as much polyunsaturated fat present to saturated fat. P:M:S ratio is the ratio of polyunsaturated to monounsaturated to saturated fat.

PRESERVATIVES
Preservatives are food additives approved under government regulations to control the growth of mould, bacteria and yeasts in order to increase the shelf life of foods. Canned, frozen and dried foods do not need preservatives as the process itself is the preserving agent, restricting access of oxygen or water so the 'bugs' can't grow. Where preservatives are used they are listed in the food's ingredient list by name or food additive number.

PROCESSED FOODS
Most food requires some sort of processing before it is eaten. Peeling an apple, cooking a chicken and making a custard in the home is all food processing. Much of the food processing today is done by large manufacturers in factories using many processes similar to those done at home. Commercially processed foods are covered by strict regulations to ensure they are safe and wholesome. Processing is essential in modern-day life to ensure a

wide selection of foods throughout the year, to stop or slow contamination of foods by bacteria, to increase storage life, to make food appetizing and to reduce time spent in preparation.

PUBERTY

Refers to the series of physical and physiological changes that turn children into adults capable of reproducing. The onset of puberty varies from child to child but most girls start about 11 years (range 9–13 years) while boys are generally later, starting at 12 years (range 9–14 years). Puberty normally takes between 2 and 5 years.

Some of the changes to expect during puberty are:

- A rapid growth spurt accompanied by a good appetite. Often a child never seems to be satisfied and can 'eat you out of house and home'. Good nutrition is important during this time. Important nutrients are protein, iron, zinc and calcium.
- Maturation of the sexual organs and the appearance of the secondary sexual characteristics (e.g. breasts, pubic hair).
- Shape changes. In girls, hips get rounder and wider as they put on more fat. Before puberty about 20–24% of a girl's body weight is made up of fat. After puberty this has increased to 28%. Boys, on the other hand, actually lose fat as they become more muscular. At the beginning of puberty 17–20% of a boy's weight is from fat, whereas after puberty this has fallen to 10–12%. Changes also occur in the shape of the face, which lengthens, and the lower jaw gets bigger.

RESTRAINED EATING

Restrained eating is a mild eating disorder in which food intake is intentionally restricted in order to maintain weight. Restrained eaters deny hunger and avoid situations where food is involved, such as parties or going out to dinner. They don't eat between-meal snacks, avoid fat, and eat only a limited range of foods. It has been suggested that this type of eating could lead to anorexia and bulimia. While it is common mostly in young women, it may also be a problem with children who are concerned about their weight.

RECOMMENDED DIETARY INTAKES (RDIs)

RDIs are the intakes of essential vitamins, minerals and kilojoules considered necessary to meet the requirements of groups of healthy infants, children, adolescents and adults. They are decided by expert scientific committees. Each country publishes its own RDIs. Australian RDIs are available from government bookshops and health and nutrition departments.

RIBOFLAVIN

Also known as vitamin B2, riboflavin has an important role in protein and carbohydrate metabolism and is needed for growth, general health and repair of tissues. A deficiency can lead to a sore red tongue, eye problems and cracks in the corners of the mouth. Dairy products such as milk, yoghurts and cheeses are the best sources. Other sources are liver, yeast extracts, lean meat, eggs, breakfast cereals, broccoli and almonds.

ROYAL JELLY

Royal jelly is regarded as a health tonic or miracle cure for a number of conditions. It is a white substance, rich in protein, from the glands of worker bees. It is fed to all bee larvae for three days after birth and subsequently only to those chosen to be queen bees. Following reports of 11 cases of allergic reactions to royal jelly and one death of an 11 year old girl, all Australian health products with royal jelly must carry a warning on the label that it can cause severe allergic reactions in allergy and asthma sufferers. So if your child suffers from asthma or has allergies, avoid royal jelly.

SALICYLATES

These are naturally occurring chemicals found in many fruits (apples, apricots, blackberries, cherries, peaches, oranges, mandarins), vegetables (carrots, new and red potatoes, pumpkins, turnips, corn, zucchini, cauliflowers), nuts, herbs, spices, jams, honey, yeast extracts, tea, coffee, juices, beer and wine. Salicylates are also found in perfumes, eucalyptus oils, aspirin and peppermint. They can cause unpleasant reactions in sensitive individuals if too much is eaten.

SALT

Common table salt is made up of sodium and chloride. The eating of too much salt has been associated with high blood pressure, stroke, fluid retention and heart disease. Australians currently consume about 8–12 g (1½–2½ teaspoons) a day, far in excess of the physiological requirements of ½ g a day. Most of the salt we eat comes from processed foods.

Draft Dietary Guidelines for children recommend using low-salt foods and using salt sparingly. This is not because of a relationship between salt and blood pressure in children, but because the liking for salty foods is an acquired one. It is easier for children to reduce their salt intake if they have not acquired the liking for it. Dietary Guidelines for adults also recommend a decrease in salt consumption, so the whole family should make efforts to lower salt intake.

SATURATED FATS

Saturated fats are hard fats at room temperature and are found predominantly in animal foods (meat, eggs and dairy products such as butter and cheese). Commercial shortenings used in biscuits, cakes, sauces etc. are usually saturated. Coconut fat, while a vegetable fat, contains mostly saturated fats. Saturated fats raise cholesterol and are strongly implicated in heart disease. Like all fats, saturated fats should be kept to a minimum.

SORBITOL

Sorbitol is a sugar alcohol used as a sugar substitute in low-joule foods such as jams and chocolates, and as a humectant to retain moisture in foods such as baked goods. It occurs naturally in a number of fruits but can also be made synthetically. It is about half as sweet as sucrose. Large amounts of sorbitol (about 20–50 g, or 1–2½ tablespoons) can cause bloating, gas and diarrhoea as it is not completely absorbed by the body.

SOY DRINKS (MILK)

Soy drinks are made from soya beans that have been soaked, ground, cooked and strained. They contain no lactose so are suitable for those with a lactose intolerance. Although used for cow's milk protein allergy, it is important to realise those allergic to cow's milk protein may also be allergic to soy protein.

Where soy drinks replace cow's milk it is important to use a fortified soy drink that approximates cow's milk in nutritional composition. Compared to cow's milk, unfortified soy drinks are inadequate in calcium, vitamin A, Vitamin B2 (riboflavin), Vitamin B12, the amino acid methionine, energy, protein and fat.

SPLENDA

Splenda is the brand name for sucralose, an artificial sweetener made from partially chlorinated sugar. (See also Sucralose).

STARCH

Also referred to as complex carbohydrate, it is the storage form of glucose in plants. It is found in cereal grains, breakfast cereals, pasta, noodles, rice, vegetables, unripe fruit, nuts and legumes. Starches are also added to foods to thicken them and to improve the stability of the product and the feel of them in the mouth.

Until recently starch was considered to be completely digested and absorbed by the body. We now know that at least 10% of the starch we eat is not digested but is fermented in the large bowel (colon) by bacteria. Butyrate is formed by this fermentation which promotes the formation of healthy cells and so is protective against cancer.

Starch is an important nutrient for children providing much needed energy. Cutting back on fat means that the kilojoules must be replaced. Most adults and children, when reducing fat, do not eat enough starch to replace lost energy, which leaves them short of kilojoules. Unfortunately starch still has the image of being stodgy and fattening. Replacing fat with fruits and vegetables is good, but these don't provide adequate starch for the body's needs. Encourage children to snack on starchy foods!

SUCRALOSE

Sucralose is an artificial sweetener made from partially chlorinated sugar. It is 600 times sweeter than sugar, and provides no kilojoules/calories. It can be used successfully in cooking and baking and is stable over long-term storage. Its taste is closest to sugar and it does not promote dental caries. Although artificial sweeteners are not recommended for children, studies have shown that sucralose is not hazardous in children's diets. Sucralose is used in low-joule/calorie (energy) foods and is available as a sugar replacement in powdered form. Its brand name is Splenda.

SUGARS

Sugars are carbohydrates supplying 16 kilojoules (4 calories) a gram, half that of fats. They give sweetness to food and make it more palatable. The major sugars include lactose (milk sugar), glucose (blood sugar), fructose (fruit sugar) and maltose (from cereals). They vary in sweetness, the sweetest being fructose followed by sucrose, glucose, maltose and lactose.

Children have a natural liking for sweet foods. As we get older our preference for sweet food declines and we increase our liking for more savoury foods.

Sugars can be an ideal vehicle for getting children to eat nutritious foods they don't like and so wouldn't normally eat. Examples: milk — add flavouring; water — add a small amount of fruit juice or cordial; breakfast cereal — use sweeter cereal varieties or add a small amount of sugar.

Too much sugar in the diet can cause tooth decay and contribute to overweight and obesity. Added sugars — particularly in soft drinks, cordials, confectionery, biscuits, jams and cakes — should be kept to a minimum.

SULPHUR DIOXIDE

Sulphur dioxide is used as a preservative and anti-oxidant in food. May be added as sulphur dioxide, or as sulphite, bisulphite or metabisulphite. It is added to fruit drinks, dried fruit, soft drinks, fresh fruit salads, beer, wine, and sausages. Reactions to sulphur dioxide have occurred in some sensitive individuals, and include nausea, diarrhoea and asthma.

TASTE

How a food tastes determines whether a child will eat it. Children universally prefer sweet-tasting foods and dislike bitter or sour foods but this preference for sweet food tends to decline as they get older.

Children are often wary of new tastes, and this is perfectly natural. They need time to become familiar with taste (sweetness, sourness, bitterness) and flavour (taste plus aroma). While flavour and taste are important in food acceptance, so is the influence of the peer group; that is, children will be influenced by what their friends are eating. (See also Chapter Three.)

TARTRAZINE

Tartrazine is a synthetic yellow colour added to custard mixes, snack foods, confectionery, sauces and desserts. Controversy has surrounded its use as it has been associated with asthma and hyperactivity in children. However, the number of people with tartrazine sensitivity is very small and in general it is considered safe for use.

TEA

Tea is a popular beverage made from Camellia sinensis, a plant which grows in tropical and subtropical regions. Tea contains caffeine (a cup of tea has approximately 30–50 g/1–1¾ oz of caffeine) and tannins. Tannins can interfere with the absorption of iron. Weak tea contains less caffeine and tannins than strong tea.

While not generally recommended as a beverage for children, weak tea is well-liked. For children 6–17 years tea appears to be a major source of dietary caffeine, but in amounts well below acceptable levels of intake. (See also Caffeine, Herbal teas.)

TEETH

See Chapter Four.

THIAMINE

Also called vitamin B1, thiamine is necessary for the body to convert carbohydrates to energy. It is needed for the functioning of the brain, nervous system and heart. Thiamine needs are related to energy requirements. The more kilojoules/calories ingested, the greater the requirement for thiamine. Good sources are lean pork, wholegrain cereals and bread, breakfast cereals, infant cereals, yeast extracts, liver and kidney.

TRANS FATTY ACIDS
See Fatty acids.

UNDERWEIGHT
Children are underweight when their weight is less than what is suitable for their height. Often children who are described by their parents as 'underweight' are not: they just happen to be thin and small or tall, probably a common feature in the family. Providing they eat well and are growing and developing normally, there is no need to worry. See your dietitian or doctor if you are concerned.

A child who is consistently thin and not growing needs attention. This could be due to an emotional problem, an underlying illness or poor diet. Failure to grow and being underweight are seen in children whose parents unnecessarily restrict foods to prevent their children being overweight; such parents encourage low-fat, very high-fibre food and disallow healthy snacks. Vegetarian, particularly vegan children can be at risk.

VEGETARIAN DIETS
There are three types of vegetarian diets:
- Vegan, which excludes all foods of animal origin.
- Lactovegetarian, which includes dairy products but excludes meat, poultry, fish, eggs.
- Ovo-lactovegetarian, which excludes all meat, poultry and fish but includes milk and egg dishes.

These diets, with the exception of vegan, are healthy for children provided foods are selected appropriately. Vegan diets may be lacking in Vitamin B12, iron, calcium and zinc, which can affect growth and development.

Dietary Guidelines for a vegetarian diet include eating the following foods:
- Legumes (soy, kidney, navy beans etc.), lentils, nuts, seeds and eggs
- Milk and milk products (including calcium-fortified soy products)
- Cereal grains, breakfast cereals, bread, rice, pasta, noodles
- Fruits and vegetables
- Margarine, butter, oil in small quantities

(See also Chapter Nine on vegetarian food ideas.)

VITAMIN AND MINERAL SUPPLEMENTS
Supplements are not necessary for healthy, growing children who eat a well-balanced diet. However, groups that may be at risk include vegetarian children (iron, zinc), children who have suffered long or numerous illnesses, children who do not eat any dairy foods or appropriate substitutes such as calcium-fortified soy drinks or goat's milk. Consult with your doctor or dietitian if you feel vitamin and mineral supplements are needed. When selecting supplements choose only those designed for children so that the appropriate levels of nutrients are given. (See also Chapter Six.)

VITAMINS
Vitamins are essential for life, being involved in all the various chemical reactions that occur in the body, such as the processing of other nutrients (proteins, fats, carbohydrates and minerals), formation of blood cells, hormones, genes and nervous system chemicals. They are required in only very small amounts.

There are 13 known vitamins divided into two groups: water soluble (B group and C) and fat soluble (vitamins A, D, E, K). A deficiency of a vitamin upsets the body's metabolism and causes symptoms. Excess of certain vitamins, particularly the fat soluble vitamins, can be harmful.

For more on vitamin A, see Beta carotene; on vitamin B1, see Thiamine; on vitamin B2, see Riboflavin; on vitamin B3, see Niacin; on vitamin C, see Ascorbic acid; on vitamin K, see K, vitamin.

WATER

Water is essential for our survival. Our bodies are 60% water and it is needed to maintain fluid balance, for chemical reactions to transport substances in and out of cells, and for the body's secretions (such as digestive juices) and excretions (urine, sweat). Children require about 1–1½ litres/48 fl oz per day. Water comes not only from what we drink but also from foods (e.g. bread contains 40% water, fruit 80–90% water, beef 62% water) and from the breakdown of proteins, carbohydrates and fats in the body.

WEIGHT REDUCTION

Weight reduction diets are not recommended for children. These diets may put nutrients at risk and cause children distress. For overweight children the aim is to prevent weight gain or to maintain current weight, not to reduce weight. As the child grows taller, holding weight constant will bring him into the ideal weight range. Overweight children should be treated like other children and given a healthy diet with snacks, avoiding high-fat and sugar foods and encouraging plenty of exercise.

Best results are obtained with children whose family give support and follow a healthy eating plan, keeping high-fat, high-sugar snacks, confectionery etc. out of the house so they won't be a temptation.

If the child is very obese, dieting should be under the supervision of a dietitian. (See also Fat children, Obesity, Fats, Carbohydrates.)

XYLITOL

Xylitol is a sweetener that is produced commercially from wood but also found naturally in fruits and vegetables. It does not cause tooth decay. Like mannitol and sorbitol it can cause diarrhoea if taken in excess.

YEAST

Yeast is a single-cell living organism related to fungi such as moulds and mushrooms. Brewer's yeast and baker's yeast are the two main types of yeast. Yeast ferments sugar to become carbon dioxide and alcohol. Yeasts are a good source of protein, have little fat and sugar, and are rich sources of B vitamins except vitamin B12. They are also high in the minerals potassium, phosphorous, iron, chromium, zinc, selenium, magnesium and calcium.

Reactions to yeast and yeast-containing foods occur in some sensitive children. As yeasts also contain salicylates and amines, common natural chemicals causing food sensitive reactions, a diet avoiding just yeast and moulds may not get rid of symptoms.

YEAST EXTRACTS

These are black salty spreads used on bread and also in recipes to boost flavours in recipes. They are excellent sources of B vitamins but tend to be quite salty.

YOGHURT

A popular food or dessert, yoghurt is made from pasteurised cow's milk or skim milk. Milk is mixed with cultures of lactobacillus and streptococcus thermophilus and held at 45°C (110°F) until it thickens. It is then cooled, flavoured and sweetened as required.

The yoghurt cultures break down lactose (milk sugar) to lactic acid, giving yoghurt its characteristic acid taste. This conversion also makes yoghurt suitable for some people with lactose intolerance. Yoghurt has the same nutritional properties as milk.

Yoghurts using cultures lactobacillus acidophilus and bifidobacterium are becoming popular. (See also Acidophilus.)

ZINC

Zinc is an important mineral found in lean meat, chicken, cheese, nuts, oysters and liver. It is important for the body to enable it to use proteins and carbohydrates, and is essential for wound healing and good vision. Lack of zinc can cause a loss of appetite and taste. Lack of zinc in children affects growth and sexual maturity.

INDEX

RECIPE INDEX

Also by Anne Hillis and Penelope Stone

BREAST, BOTTLE, BOWL

An invaluable, commonsense guide which takes all the anxiety and mystery out of feeding babies and young children. Instead of complex prescriptions for nutrient quantities and vitamin intakes, it gives sound, practical advice in a form that all parents will find easy to follow. It shows how the apparently daunting question of a good diet really can take care of itself, with a basic understanding of nutrition and a few simple guidelines.

BREAST, BOTTLE, BOWL encourages an enjoyable, stress-free approach to feeding babies and very young children, including information on:

- *successful breast feeding*

- *weaning and bottle feeding*

- *introducing solids*

- *hygiene in food preparation*

- *reasonable expectations about quantities*

- *coping with fussy eaters and food refusal*

- *delicious, fuss-free recipes*